Concise Introduction to Global Supply Chain Management

Elgar Concise Introductions are inspiring and considered introductions to the key principles in business, expertly written by some of the world's leading scholars. The aims of the series are twofold: to pinpoint essential principles of business and management, and to offer insights that stimulate critical thinking. By distilling the subject into a concise and meaningful form, the books serve as accessible introductions for graduate and undergraduate students coming to the subject for the first time. Importantly, they also develop well-informed, nuanced critiques of the field that will challenge and extend the understanding of advanced students, scholars and thinking practitioners.

For a full list of Edward Elgar published titles, including the titles in this series, visit our website at www.e-elgar.com.

Concise Introduction to

Global Supply Chain Management

MASAAKI KOTABE

Professor, School of Commerce, Waseda University, Japan, and the Shidler College of Business, University of Hawaii at Manoa, USA

Elgar Concise Introductions

Edward Elgar
PUBLISHING

Cheltenham, UK • Northampton, MA, USA

Published by
Edward Elgar Publishing Limited
The Lypiatts
15 Lansdown Road
Cheltenham
Glos GL50 2JA
UK

Edward Elgar Publishing, Inc.
William Pratt House
9 Dewey Court
Northampton
Massachusetts 01060
USA

A catalogue record for this book
is available from the British Library

Library of Congress Control Number: 2023952679

This book is available electronically in the **Elgar**online
Business subject collection
http://dx.doi.org/10.4337/9781800372894

ISBN 978 1 80037 288 7 (cased)
ISBN 978 1 80037 289 4 (eBook)
ISBN 978 1 80037 290 0 (paperback)

Printed and bound in Great Britain by
TJ Books Limited, Padstow, Cornwall

To Lorraine, Akie, Euka, Hiro, Kai and Cam, who continue to enrich my life.

Contents

About the author

Masaaki "Mike" Kotabe holds a joint appointment at the School of Commerce, Waseda University in Tokyo, Japan and at the Shidler College of Business at the University of Hawaii at Manoa in the United States. Previously, he held the Washburn Chair Professorship at the Fox School of Business at Temple University from 1998–2021 and the Ambassador Edward Clark Centennial Endowed Fellow and Professorship in Marketing and International Business at the University of Texas at Austin from 1990–98.

Dr. Kotabe was elected a Fellow of the Academy of International Business (AIB) in 1998 and a Fellow of the Japan Academy of International Business Studies in 2017 for his significant contribution to international business research and education. He served as President of the Academy of International Business in 2016–17 and as Editor of the *Journal of International Management* from 2002–19. He has written more than 150 schol-

arly publications, including many in leading journals, as well as more than 20 books. Most recently, he received a Gold Medalist award from the AIB as one of the most published researchers in the world over the past 50 years in the *Journal of International Business Studies* in 2019.

Figures

Tables

Preface

Global supply chain management has gradually gained academic attention since the mid-1980s. Today, it has grown into a prominent area of study at business schools around the world. Over the years, however, different terms have been used to characterize this area of study – including "global logistics," "sourcing," "purchasing," "procurement" and "physical distribution" – which emphasize different aspects of what is now referred to as the "global supply chain." As such, "global supply chain" is an amalgam that encompasses all areas of business related to the movement of materials and other inputs through production and physical distribution of products to the final customer. In the past, this used to be a straightforward mechanism of throughput managed by a firm: the firm would purchase materials and convert them through its manufacturing process into a finished product for final distribution and sale to buyers.

Internationally, this was characterized as exports and imports. Over time, in addition to exporting, firms began to set up assembly operations in foreign markets with materials and components brought from their home countries for the sale of finished products in those local markets. This was sometimes – and somewhat pejoratively – called "screwdriver operation." Firms gradually started exporting finished products to third-world countries as well as back to their home countries. Sometimes, the suppliers of those materials and components followed the principal firms abroad and set up their own production in foreign markets to stay close to their customers. Alternatively, principal firms began to procure necessary materials and components from local suppliers in foreign markets. Taken to the extreme, some foreign manufacturing firms began procuring all necessary materials and components in their local markets. For example, this would be the case if Toyota – a Japanese manufacturer – procured all materials and components from U.S. domestic suppliers for its production in the United States for eventual automobile sales in the United States.

Initially, the research and development for designing and developing high-tech materials and components was handled in-house by principal firms and their major suppliers. Over time, however, the global dispersal of these activities led to the study of global sourcing strategies. In other words, the research and managerial focus used to be on how firms managed all these activities within their corporate system. Today, we may call this "insourcing."

However, starting from the 1990s, these manufacturing firms increasingly began to rely on independent suppliers to design and produce technology-rich materials and components for them. In other words, attention gradually shifted to how best to manage "outsourcing," or the procurement of major materials and components from independent suppliers both at home and abroad. Sometimes, those principal manufacturing firms and independent suppliers established joint development strategies under long-term contractual arrangements, joint ventures or licensing agreements. The contractual relationships between principal manufacturing firms and their suppliers have added further complexity to business transactions. Just think of Apple, a U.S.-based company widely known for its iPhones. Apple designs the iPhone's technological architecture but it does not have its own efficient manufacturing capabilities; instead, it relies on Taiwan-based Foxconn not only to engineer the physical layout of high-tech computer chips and sensors produced by, say, the Taiwan Semiconductor Manufacturing Company (TSMC), another Taiwanese company, and Sony, a Japanese company, but also to assemble the actual iPhones in China for distribution and marketing in various parts of the world. Moreover, this arrangement does not involve a one-way technical and technological influence from Apple to Foxconn: increasingly, Foxconn is advising Apple on new and more effective iPhone architecture.[1] Finally, Apple relies on independent distributors as well as its own Apple stores for marketing around the world.

The global supply chain covers the gamut of activities involved in the complex manufacture and sale of final products, with an emphasis on the

---

[1] "Foxconn, Apple and the Partnership that Changed the Tech Sector," Nikkei Asia, July 13, 2017, https://asia.nikkei.com/.

designs and flows of materials into, through and out of firms on a global basis. In this book, we focus on how to manage the global supply chain to achieve firms' corporate objectives at a minimum total cost.

In a way, global supply chain management as a subject differs from conventional business subjects such as finance, manufacturing, marketing and human resource management, because it deals with "boundary issues" that cut across all aspects of business management. Learning and knowing about one of these conventional business subjects alone would not make it possible for us to manage a firm; but at the same time, learning and knowing about all business subjects not only would be too daunting a task but also would leave us suffering from "Jack of all trades, master of none" syndrome. However, it is knowledge of these boundary issues that ties all of these different aspects of business together to work coherently.

As such, global supply chain management is a broad but unique area of business to learn about. I was lucky enough to become interested in this topic as it was emerging in the 1980s. Over the last 40-plus years, while I led this research area, I was blessed with the opportunity to work with young researchers who continued our research together. Condensing these decades of research into a relatively short book was equally daunting. Although I cannot list all the names of my collaborators, I am particularly grateful to Janet Y. Murray (University of Missouri-St. Louis), Michael J. Mol (Copenhagen Business School) and Ronaldo Parente (Florida International University) for their insights and inspiration through our joint writings over the years. As such, this book represents the results of our collective efforts, not just mine.

Finally, I am delighted to share our research results and experience with you through this book. Our teaching experience is an amalgam of our own learning and knowledge gained through continued discussions with our colleagues, students and executive friends.

1 Introduction to *Global Supply Chain Management*

Introduction

What is global supply chain management? First, the word "global" reflects the competitive pressures and market opportunities that arise around the world today and a firm's need to optimize its market performance on a global basis. Whether a firm operates domestically or across national boundaries, it can no longer avoid these influences from all corners of the world. For optimal market performance, a firm should also be ready and willing to take advantage of resources on a global basis and to respond to different needs and wants of consumers. In a way, global business involves a constant balancing act between the economies of scale and scope needs of the firm on one hand, and its responsiveness and sensitivity to different market conditions on the other. While some people call this a "glocal" ("global" + "local") orientation, we retain the term "global" to emphasize operational flexibility to address similarities and differences on a global basis.

So, what is supply chain management? Imagine a typical U.S. company exporting finished products to Europe and Japan. In a traditional textbook, this export activity would be treated as a bilateral business transaction between a U.S. company and foreign customers. In reality, however, in the minds of the executives of the U.S. company, this export transaction may represent the last phase of the activities they manage. Say the company procures high-tech components from long-term partner suppliers in Japan; other crucial components through a business-to-business (B2B) transaction with suppliers in China under license with another U.S. company; and additional software from its U.S.-based suppliers through a joint venture with a German company operating in India. The finished product is assembled in a Chinese plant owned by a Taiwanese contract manufacturer for export to various countries, including the United States. In other words, this particular export transaction by the U.S. company involves business partnerships, a licensing agreement, a joint venture, B2B transactions with suppliers, local assembly and research and development – all managed directly or indirectly by the U.S. company.

Today, the management of these complex intertwined activities is called "global supply chain management." This is a relatively new term, as we will explain later. We emphasize this multilateral realism by examining these value-adding activities as holistically as possible. In a way, global supply chain management constitutes all operational aspects of the manufacturing business; but it focuses more on physical movements, ranging from materials and components development and procurement to sourcing decisions and physical distribution of finished products on a global basis.

Why global supply chain management is important

Companies must deliver products to customers both *efficiently* and *effectively*.[1] "Efficiency" refers to cost efficiency, while "effectiveness" refers to customer satisfaction. First, global supply chain management – also commonly referred to as "global logistics management" – has played a critical role in the growth and development of world trade and the integration of business operations on a global scale. Its primary objective is to develop a cost-efficient delivery mechanism to meet the needs of customers. In fact, the level of world trade in goods and, to some extent, services depends to a significant degree on the availability of economical and reliable international transportation and logistics services. Decreases in transportation costs and increases in performance reliability expand the scope of business operations and increase the associated level of international trade and competition.[2] Second, the use of appropriate

---

[1]   For a philosophy of efficiency versus effectiveness-seeking in business orientation, see Masaaki Kotabe, "Efficiency vs. Effectiveness Orientation of Global Sourcing Strategy: A Comparison of U.S. and Japanese Multinational Companies," *Academy of Management Executive*, 12, November 1998: 107–19; Shelby D. Hunt and Dale F. Duhan, "Competition in the Third Millennium: Efficiency or Effectiveness?" *Journal of Business Research*, 55, February 2002: 97–102.

[2]   John H. Dunning, "Reappraising the Eclectic Paradigm in an Age of Alliance Capitalism," *Journal of International Business Studies*, 26, Third Quarter 1995: 461–91.

distribution channels in international markets dramatically increases the chances of success. The primary objective is to develop a task-effective delivery mechanism for customer satisfaction.

U.S. Army General Omar Bradley, who was the first chairperson of the U.S. Joint Chiefs of Staff and oversaw the U.S. military's policy-making during the Korean War (1950–53), once famously offered that: "Amateurs talk strategy. Professionals talk logistics."[3] This clearly highlights the importance of logistics in winning a war. But as far back as 1954, Peter Drucker – probably the most prominent business thinker of the twentieth century – also decried that logistics would remain "the darkest continent of business"[4]; and his prediction proved true well into the twenty-first century. It is not too difficult to demonstrate the importance of the physical handling, movement, storage and retrieval of materials and products.

For almost every product, more than 50 percent of the product cost is material related, while less than 10 percent is labor related. Yet over the years, this fact has received little attention. For three consecutive years, from 2006 to 2008, the U.S. total logistics cost stayed at nearly 10 percent of gross domestic product (GDP). More recently, it was 7.6 percent in 2019 and 7.4 percent in 2020.[5] Clearly, logistical operations have become more efficient in the United States over the years. On the other hand, logistics spending in China was roughly equivalent to 15 percent of GDP in 2016. China was able to cut logistics costs by $14 billion, or 0.12 percent of GDP, in 2017 to relieve the burden on business. On the other hand, India's logistics sector is highly fragmented, with the cost currently standing at 14 percent of GDP; although the government is seeking to reduce this figure.[6]

---

[3]   "U.S. Now Relies on Alternate Afghan Supply Routes," *National Public Radio*, www.NPR.com, September 16, 2011.

[4]   Peter F. Drucker, *The Practice of Management* (New York: Harper & Brothers, 1954).

[5]   "The State of the Logistics Union 2021," *Supply Chain Digest*, www.scdigest .com, June 25, 2021.

[6]   "China Cuts $14 Billion in Logistics Costs in 2017," *China Daily*, www .chinadaily.com, February 8, 2018; "India Aiming to Reduce Logistics Cost to Less Than 10% Of GDP by 2022," *Business Standard*, www.business -standard.com, August 24, 2018.

Since the 1990s, a variety of issues have driven the increased emphasis on global supply chain management. This was epitomized in 1998 by General Motors' lawsuit against Volkswagen over the defection of José Ignacio Lopez, the former vice president of purchasing at General Motors and one of the most renowned logistics managers in the automobile industry.[7] His expertise is said to have saved General Motors several billion dollars on its purchasing and logistics operations, which directly affected the company's bottom line. The importance of distribution channels is further evidenced by recent mergers in the auto industry, in which giant multinationals have gobbled up smaller manufacturers with strong brand names but inadequate global distribution, such as the acquisition of Volvo from Ford by China's Geely.[8]

As firms start operating on a global basis, global supply chain/logistics managers need to manage the procurement and shipping of materials, components and supplies to various manufacturing sites at the most economical and reliable rates. Simultaneously, these firms need to ship finished goods to customers in markets around the world at the desired place and time. The development of intermodal transportation and electronic tracking technology has boosted the efficiency of the logistics methods employed by firms. "Intermodal transportation" refers to the seamless transfer of goods from one mode of transport (e.g., aircraft or ship) to another (e.g., truck) and vice versa without the hassle of unpacking and repackaging the goods to suit the dimensions of the mode of transport being used. "Tracking technology" refers to the means of keeping continuous tabs on the exact location of the goods being shipped in the supply chain – this enables quick responses to any disruption in shipments because the shipper knows exactly where the goods are in real time and alternative means can be quickly mobilized.

However, we have also begun to realize that the pursuit of economic efficiency alone may not be optimal for society as a whole. Supply chain management as we know it today has been based on a "linear economy" paradigm (i.e., make, use and dispose), in which the primary role of firms is to develop, manufacture and distribute products downstream to final consumers at a minimum total cost. Given the increased urgency of

---

[7]   "No Ordinary Car Thief," *U.S. News & World Report*, June 5, 2000, p. 52.

[8]   "Geely Buys Volvo. Believe It or Not, It Could Work," *Bloomberg Businessweek*, March 29, 2010.

warnings against climate change and environmental pollution in recent decades, we also need to think of ways for firms to reduce this one-way resource. This could be done by building a circular closed supply chain loop, so that products which are at the end of their service life are recycled into resources for others to minimize resource inputs and reduce waste, pollution and carbon emissions.

The aim of this book

This book is intended to help the reader become more knowledgeable about the issues involved in the global supply chain, rather than merely its management. By enhancing their awareness of these issues, global supply chain managers[9] and aspiring managers can better educate and position themselves to tackle various problems as they build their careers in supply chain management. As such, this book is designed more to offer "food for thought" than to provide technical "tools of management." The technically inclined are encouraged to consult more advanced technical books.

This book aims to explain global supply chain management based on some of the best and most interesting research work on it that cuts across international business and international management, marketing, strategic management, operations and purchasing management and economics. While some of these research areas may appear unrelated, this broad array reflects the multi-disciplinary, boundary-spanning nature of global supply chain management.[10] Global supply chain management should be examined from a strategy perspective, as it affects the competitive advantage of a firm. Likewise, it has much to do with marketing, as these supply chains are designed to serve customers around the world. Economic theory helps explain why certain supply chain structures gain

---

[9]   Supply chain managers may have various other job titles, including "supplier quality engineer," "technical buyer," "director of supplier management," "procurement manager," "logistics manager," "transportation manager," "distribution manager," "production planning manager," "production manager" or "operations manager." These managers cover some if not all aspects of supply chain management.

[10]   For readers interested in technical academic writings, see, for example, Masaaki Kotabe and Michael J. Mol, *Global Supply Chain Management* (Northampton, MA: Edward Elgar Publishing, 2006).

traction and others do not. From an operational perspective, global supply chain management poses challenges to the way operations are organized and managed. Lastly, scholars of international business and international management are primarily concerned with two questions. First, what causes firms to expand internationally – in this case by globalizing their supply base – and what management challenges does this practice present? Second, how do firms from and in various countries differ in their supply chain management practices? What explanations can we provide for those differences and what are the consequences for the management of global supply chains?

The book is organized as follows. In Chapter 2, we offer a historical overview of how global supply chain management has evolved to become a separate business discipline, much like marketing, finance, accounting and so on. This has not come out of the blue, however. Global supply chain management is a human endeavor. If you think something is important, it will become an important issue. If, on the other hand, you do not think it warrants much attention, it will be ignored or neglected. Such competing thoughts have eventually transformed the logic of "moving things" into the discipline of global supply chain management that we know today. In the process, different terms have been coined to describe the phenomenon and are still in use today. However, over the years, the topic of global supply chain management has been seen as more salient and vital to business success in a highly globalized competitive market.

Global supply chain management consists of materials procurement and sourcing strategy (upstream activities), and physical distribution (downstream activities). Chapter 3 discusses materials procurement and sourcing strategy, as they are practically inseparable parts of global supply chain management. The focus is on "where" to procure materials and components from, and "how" to do so on a global basis. In a way, it involves a complex set of "make" or "buy" decisions involving both suppliers and own firms across national boundaries in various arrangements, including licensing, strategic alliances and subsidiaries. Naturally, political, legal and cultural issues become intertwined with these activities.

Chapter 4 focuses on the performance implications of sourcing strategy. This has been a core focus of global supply chain management over the years, as "make" or "buy" decisions (known as "insourcing" versus "outsourcing") ultimately determine the boundary of the firm – that is, how much it should invest in performing various value-adding activities within the corporate system to achieve and maintain competitive advantage. There is no straightforward answer to the performance implications of sourcing strategy. Rather, it requires a balancing act between the advantages and disadvantages of various issues involved in sourcing strategy.

Chapter 5 offers a historical view of the dynamic effects of insourcing versus outsourcing decisions on three global electronics companies from the United States, Europe and Japan over time. We tend to look at this issue through a static "snapshot" view of the recent past. However, firms' strategy and the industry itself evolve over time due to competition, technological and market changes, and changes in the financial and political environment, among other things. Therefore, global supply chain management must also be examined from a long-term "dynamic" perspective. History always gives us a good understanding of trends and patterns over a long period and provides us with lessons to learn from, and think about, for the future.

Chapter 6 focuses on the physical distribution of products. This is one of the most important aspects of marketing strategy,[11] as it deals with the vital links between production and the delivery of products to customers. The chapter covers a broad range of topics, including available modes of transportation; the growing popularity of third-party logistics by specialized logistics companies; the increased use of the internet and technological advances such as blockchain technology and the Internet of Things to improve logistics efficiency; and foreign trade zones that offer various tax benefits and marketing flexibility across national boundaries. It also covers marketing channel configurations and international retail as the last key leg of physical distribution to end customers. Finally, we are all aware that the environmental pollution and climate change that have resulted from industrial activities on a global scale in the twentieth century have called into question the sustainability of current business practices in the twenty-first century. As a result, the sustainability of current business practices is under scrutiny as we become increasingly aware of the negative effect of economic activities on the planet. To conserve and recycle limited natural resources, we need to shift gradually

---

[11] Generally, marketing strategy involves the management of activities relating to product, price, promotion, and place (commonly referred to as the "4Ps").

from a linear economy paradigm (i.e., make, use and dispose) to a circular economy paradigm (i.e., make, reuse, remake and recycle). Global supply chain management has a major role to play in addressing the sustainability issue for years to come. Chapter 7 reveals that we have just begun to scratch the surface and much more needs to be done to develop ways to design global supply chains in a more sustainable way.

By the end of the book, you will come to realize that global supply chain management encompasses all aspects of business; and that its focus is primarily on the efficient movement of materials and products through networks of firms and suppliers – not only for customer satisfaction, but increasingly to reduce wasteful resource use on a global basis.

2 A brief history of supply chain management

Introduction

In Chapter 1, we highlighted that companies must deliver products to customers both *efficiently* and *effectively*. Visualize the supply and demand curves that you may have seen in a basic economics class: where the downward-sloping demand curve and the upward-sloping supply curve meet at a cross point, the market price is determined. However, the actual marketplace is much more complex, with myriad consumers that want different features in a product and myriad companies trying to sell their own unique products with different features and characteristics. Naturally, products with more technically and aesthetically appealing features command higher prices (i.e., consumers are willing to pay a premium); while products with simple features tend to be lower priced. Unlike the simple supply and demand curves of economists, the market reality reveals the much more complex nature of supply and demand conditions.

The close historical link between marketing and supply chain management

A number of notable events occurred over the last 100 years or so before the phrase "supply chain management" became a widely accepted term. First, at the dawn of the twentieth century, the term "marketing" came into use for the first time as a management concept to explain the complexities of supply and demand in a business situation. One of the earliest authors to use the term was L.D.H. Weld, a young institutional economist at the University of Minnesota who was "very anxious to develop a knowledge of how Minnesota products were marketed."[1] This involved various activities such as collecting, sorting, inventorying, distributing, negotiating, transporting, advertising and pricing. Weld went on to author a book on the distribution of farm products. However, whenever economists heard the term "distribution," they automatically thought of income distribution. As an economist, Weld was ill advised to call his book *Distribution of Farm Products*, as it would otherwise have been called in layperson's terms. But he struggled to come up with a proper title. Aware that he was studying the dynamic aspects and processes of the marketplace for farm products transported and distributed from Minnesota – with product warranties, customer service, pricing, advertising, packaging and so on along the way – he coined the term "marketing." Back then, "market" was a noun, synonymous with "marketplace." By adding "-ing" to the noun, Weld sought to stress the dynamic processes of marketplace activities. Consequently, Weld titled his book *Marketing of Farm Products*. Published in 1916, this was one of the first books ever to use the term "marketing."[2] In later years, those marketing-related activities were neatly categorized into the now-familiar "four Ps" (product, price, promotion and place) of marketing, popularized by Jerome McCarthy in 1960 in his book *Basic Marketing: A Managerial Approach*.[3]

Why are we discussing the original concept of marketing here? As you can see, Weld's concept of marketing had a lot to do with McCarthy's fourth "P" – place, or, more contemporaneously stated, the distribution and logistics involved in selling farm products. In other words, 100-plus years ago, "marketing" mostly referred to what today is known as "distribution and logistics."

Second, in the years following the Second World War, business schools were established at many universities in the United States. Marketing was now considered one of the major functions of business and the marketing department became one of the central pillars of business schools. The marketing department's natural focus used to be on distribution and logistics. However, in those early days of business schools, professors

---

[1]   L.D.H. Weld, "Early Experience in Teaching Courses in Marketing," *Journal of Marketing*, 5(4), April 1, 1941.

[2]   L.D.H. Weld, *Marketing of Farm Products* (New York: MacMillan, 1916).

[3]   E. Jerome McCarthy, *Basic Marketing: A Managerial Approach* (Chicago, IL: Irwin, 1960).

in other more established academic disciplines – such as philosophy, mathematics, psychology, physics and chemistry – criticized business disciplines as not being scientific enough. Subsequently, business schools realized that they would need to make business disciplines, including marketing, more scientific by applying more rigorous quantitative statistical tools to the analysis of business data.[4] As a result, from the 1970s onward, areas of business research in which large amounts of quantitative data could be collected and analyzed with relative ease became more popular among younger business professors. Logistics was not considered an easy subject to theorize and analyze quantitatively and thus began to lose its popularity as a "scientific" research area. Instead, research areas such as consumer behavior (psychological) and promotion research, which afforded easier access to consumer data, increased in popularity. When one casually thinks of "marketing" today, one tends to think first of consumer behavior and promotional activities. In marketing academia, these consumer-related research areas became dominant and logistics was relegated to a second-class position. Consequently, at some leading business schools, the marketing department was relabeled as the department of "marketing and distribution," "marketing and transportation," or "marketing and logistics." However, the "classic" marketing areas (i.e., promotion and consumer behavior) dominated in those departments. The two subdisciplines, with different cultures and orientations, did not mix well, just like oil and vinegar. Thus, a separation was bound to occur.

Finally, at several business schools in the 1980s and 1990s, the distribution/logistics group broke away from the marketing department either to join the more broadly defined management department or to establish a standalone logistics department. This separation coincided with the growing popularity of the new term "supply chain management." The term "supply chain" was coined by British logistics consultant Keith Oliver in the early 1980s. This is why many universities now have a "department of supply chain management" or a "department of logistics and supply chain management."

---

[4]   The influential report, known as the Gordon-Howell Report and published by Columbia University Press in 1959, was instrumental in sending promising young business professors to Harvard University to receive intensive training in the application of mathematics and statistics in business studies. They subsequently dispersed to many leading business schools in the United States to develop quantitative approaches to business research.

By now, it should be clear that terms such as (physical) "distribution," "logistics" and "supply chain management" are all rooted in the original conceptual foundation of the marketing discipline. Although logistics and supply chain management is now considered as a separate discipline, it is still an integral part of marketing.

The scope of global supply chain management

While the term "global supply chain management" is now in popular use, there are almost as many different definitions of the term as there are authors working in the field. However, we believe all good definitions have some common elements.

First, they distinguish the "global" from the domestic context and high-light how they differ, pointing to institutional and cultural differences among countries. Second, they argue that to "supply" implies a vertical (upstream to downstream) perspective, rather than a horizontal one. Third, they posit that a "chain" means that multiple players or actors are involved. And finally, they observe that the word "management" implies a conscious and calculated effort to shape these global supply chains. Within these restrictions, however, there is significant leeway to construct one's own terminology. In this book, we will discuss the strategies that are available to firms to manage supply chains across national boundaries, given the institutional and cultural contexts in which they operate.

The results of a recent survey of logistics costs in various European countries relative to the United States are presented in Global Viewpoint 2.1.[5] Although it is possible to attribute all cost differences to topography, customs, laws of the land and other factors, they can also reflect how efficiently or inefficiently logistics is managed in various countries and regions.

---

[5]   Adapted from Masaaki Kotabe and Kristiaan Helsen, *Global Marketing Management,* 9th ed. (Hoboken, NJ: Wiley, 2023).

Global viewpoint 2.1: Regional variations in physical distribution costs in Europe and room for improvement

The physical distribution costs in supply chain management relate to transportation, warehousing, inventory, customer service/order entry and administration. Let us make a comparison, in terms of these components, of the distribution costs between the two continents on either side of the Atlantic. The following table shows a comparison of average physical distribution costs (as a percentage of revenue) with statistics dating from around 2000.

Table 2.1   Physical distribution cost differences in the European Union and the United States

	European Union	United States
Transportation	2.79%	3.23%
Warehousing	3.03%	1.98%
Inventory	1.73%	1.93%
Customer service/order entry	0.83%	0.49%
Administration	0.79%	0.44%
Total	9.17%	8.07%

The largest disparity is in warehousing, where European costs total 3.03 percent – almost one-third of total distribution costs – compared to 1.98 percent in the United States. These expenses are the cost of both plant and field warehouses, including labor, space, direct materials and so on. Another large difference can be observed in customer service/order entry – the cost of the people, space and materials needed to take orders and handle inquiries. This stands at 0.83 percent in Europe, compared to 0.49 percent in the United States.

European governments have begun to privatize transportation services. Since January 1, 1993, the European Union has presented opportunities for reducing logistics costs and boosting efficiency. And it is not just European manufacturers but also foreign manufacturers – including those in North America – which are finding that political changes in Europe have created opportunities for greater efficiencies and lower costs in their logistics.

However, there still are many political, legal and technical issues to be settled before Europe is truly unified. Across the bloc, borders have all but disappeared with the advent of high-speed passenger trains, highways without customs posts and a single currency. Europe's state-owned telephone monopolies, electric utilities, airlines and other national franchises have all been opened to competition. However, rail freight remains a bastion of Europe's old ways – a patchwork of protected, antiquated national networks. No two European countries use the same signaling systems or electric currents for their trains. For example, trains in Britain and France run on the left side of dual-track lines, while those in the rest of Europe run on the right. Since Britain and France, however, use two different gauges of track, trains that cross their shared border along the Channel Tunnel must stop to allow each car to be lifted so that its wheels can be changed.

As a result, European industry has taken to the highways for transportation. The share of goods transported by rail with the European Union has fallen to about 14 percent today from about 32 percent in 1970. In the United States, railways account for 41 percent of freight traffic. The downside to the increase in truck transport is increased traffic congestion, which hampers efficient transportation despite the unified European economy. The most conservative estimate of the cost of traffic jams is a little over 2 percent of European gross domestic product at minimum – and it could be as high as 6 percent.

Further, with the expansion of the European Union in May 2004, traditional distribution hubs in Western and Central Europe faced tougher competition. When integrating candidate countries into EU systems and practices, the European Union must restrict access to road and rail networks in some countries for between two to three years. Meanwhile, European governments and the EU have developed programs and initiatives to reduce road congestion and encourage companies to move goods transport away from roads to facilitate important infrastructure development.

Thus, logistics managers must plan how to respond to changes as they occur. The many changes reshaping European logistics strategies include the following:

- Customs procedures: For the most part, customs checkpoints as shipments cross national borders have been eliminated. Duties and trade statistics are now strictly a matter between the originating and destination countries, and intermediate countries are no longer involved. Consequently, transit times and paperwork between EU countries – particularly for truck traffic – have been steadily reduced.

- Harmonized product standards: Prior to unification, each European country had its own manufacturing, packaging, labeling and safety standards for almost every item sold within its borders. In the European Union, pan-European harmonized standards have been developed and are replacing most of those country-by-country regulations. As a result, companies can manufacture a single version of a product for sale across the whole bloc, rather than designing and manufacturing different versions of the same item for each member state. Product harmonization allows shippers to redesign not only their distribution patterns and facilities, but also their customer-service strategies.

- Transportation deregulation: The European Commission is deregulating transportation in Europe in order to open up markets in member states to competition and eliminate conflicting regulations that impede the flow of traffic between EU countries. Deregulation promises to promote the development of efficient, cost-effective services in all modes.

- Transportation infrastructure. As in Japan and the United States, growing demand for just-in-time deliveries increases traffic and exacerbates transportation bottlenecks (particularly interregional trucking). The European Commission and individual governments are actively encouraging private development of rail and water alternatives.

Sources: "Logistics Strategies for a New Europe," *Traffic Management*, 33, August 1994: 49A; "In the Unified Europe, Shipping Freight by Rail is a Journey into the Past," *Wall Street Journal*, March 29, 1999: A1 and A8; "European Transport Policy," *Logistics & Transport Focus*, 4, July/August 2002: 40–41; "Distribution Hubs Face Competition," *Logistics and Transport Focus*, May 2004: 6.

Before moving on, we must highlight another complication with the terminology. While the term "supply chain" has become more fashionable in recent years, other terms – such as "logistics" and "sourcing" – are also used extensively. Some authors use these terms interchangeably, while others define "supply chain management" somewhat more broadly than "logistics" and "sourcing management." Although we try not to engage in this definitional debate over which functions are included in each term, the Council of Logistics Management has stated that "logistics management" typically includes upstream (inbound) and downstream (outbound) transportation management, fleet management, warehousing, materials handling, order fulfillment, logistics network design and inventory management of third-party logistics services providers. To varying degrees, the logistics function also includes procurement, production planning and scheduling, packaging and assembly, and customer service.

Another term, "(global) sourcing," is also in use in (global) supply chain management. For instance, international business scholars may be more familiar with "global sourcing" as a research area than with "global supply chain management." Although business practitioners started using the term "global sourcing" in the 1980s, there was virtually no academic work on the topic back then. Academics have previously sought to define "global sourcing strategy." As early as 1992, we defined it in one of our earliest works on global sourcing strategy as:

> [the] management of the interfaces among R&D, manufacturing, and marketing on a global basis and of logistics identifying which production units will serve which particular markets and how components will be supplied for production, such that the firm can exploit both its own advantages and the comparative advantages of various countries.[6]

Indeed, in the 1980s, firms increasingly began physically separating components procurement and production from product assembly activities to improve economic efficiency on a global scale. As assembly activities tended to be more labor and capital intensive, they were increasingly moved to lower labor-cost countries such as China (now known as "outsourcing"). On the other hand, as product components became increasingly high-tech, the ability to design and produce those components – not the downstream final assembly – was identified as a major source of competitive advantage. Firms retained those technology-rich components by producing them in-house (now known as "insourcing").

Regardless of how we define it, the work that has appeared on global sourcing has focused mostly on the extent to which (multinational) firms

---

6   Masaaki Kotabe and Glenn S. Omura, "Sourcing Strategies of European and Japanese Multinationals: A Comparison," *Journal of International Business Studies*, 20, Spring 1989: 113–30.

use internal and external sources in other countries and the performance consequences that have resulted. Contrasting this with the way in which we discuss global supply chain management in this book, it is clear "global supply chain management" is a more encompassing term than "global sourcing", since it can also include the management of foreign suppliers, the structuring of the international supply network beyond dyadic buyer-seller relationships and considerations like competition between supply chains (rather than inter-firm competition), as well as the physical distribution of finished products to customers around the world. The entire area of global supply chain management is very broad.

Supply chain management is thus an integrating function with the primary responsibility for linking major business functions and business processes within and across companies into a cohesive and high-performing business model. It includes all of the logistics management activities noted above, as well as manufacturing operations and physical distribution; and it drives the coordination of processes and activities within and across marketing, sales, product design, finance and information technology. It has been asserted that "one of the most significant paradigm shifts of modern business management is that individual businesses no longer compete as solely autonomous entities, but rather as supply chains."[7]

Thus, "global supply chain management" is defined in this book as the design and management of a system that directs and controls the flows of materials into, through and out of the firm across national boundaries to achieve its corporate objectives at a minimum total cost. As shown in Figure 2.1, the global supply chain encompasses the entire range of operations concerned with the movement of products or components, including both exports and imports simultaneously. The global supply chain, like the domestic supply chain, encompasses procurement, sourcing and (physical) distribution.[8] We can divide the flow of the global supply chain into two phases: procurement and sourcing activities are *upstream activities* before final products are produced; while physical distribution activities are *downstream activities* that relate more to the marketing activities of the firm.

---

[7]   Douglas M. Lambert and Martha C. Cooper, "Issues in Supply Chain Management," *Industrial Marketing Management,* 29(1), 2000: 65–83.

[8]   Donald J. Bowersox, David J. Closs and M. Bixby Cooper, *Supply Chain Logistics Management*, 5th ed. (New York: McGraw-Hill, 2020).

"Procurement" refers to the management of the inflow of materials, components and supplies in and through the firm. "Physical distribution"

Source: Adapted from, and expanded on, Masaaki Kotabe and Kristiaan Helsen, *Global Marketing Management,* 9th ed. (Hoboken, NJ: Wiley, 2023), p. 528.

Figure 2.1   Global supply chain management

refers to the movement of the firm's finished products to its customers, consisting of transportation, warehousing, inventory, customer service/ order entry and administration. Exporting and importing are integral parts of physical distribution. For example, a firm may export its finished products from the place of manufacture to various market locations around the world and import finished products for local sales from the place of manufacture elsewhere. "Sourcing strategy" refers to an important operational link between procurement and physical distribution, and deals with how companies manage research and development (e.g., product development and engineering), operations (e.g., manufacturing) and marketing activities; it is generally considered the most central part of supply chain management.

Although procurement activities are conceptually identified separately, they are intertwined with sourcing strategy in the whole process of developing and producing finished products. Therefore, these two upstream activities of supply chain management will be explained in tandem. However, physical distribution constitutes downstream activities involving the process of moving the finished products to end customers. These downstream activities will be explained separately.

Notably, however, both upstream and downstream activities are affected differently by the traditions, culture, economic infrastructure, laws and topography, among other things, of each country and region. In general, in geographically large countries such as the United States, where products are transported over long distances, firms tend to incur relatively higher transportation and inventory costs than those in smaller countries. On the other hand, in geographically concentrated countries, such as Japan and Britain, firms tend to incur relatively higher warehousing, customer service/order entry and general administrative costs than those in geographically larger countries. This is primarily because a wide variety of products with different features must be stored to meet the diverse needs of customers in concentrated areas.

Summary

"Supply chain management" may be a relatively new term, coined in the 1980s, but the genesis of this subject dates back to the emergence of the discipline of marketing at the dawn of the twentieth century. It used to be called "(physical) distribution" and was later recognized as the fourth "P" (place) of marketing strategy. Because it involves the relatively unglamorous and time-consuming tasks of moving materials and products, building relationships with suppliers and distributors and negotiating on prices and delivery terms, among other things; and because of the difficulties in conducting sufficiently rigorous scientific academic research, this complex and overarching subject failed to receive adequate attention from either academics or business practitioners until the 1980s.

Although terms like "logistics," "sourcing strategy" and "supply chain management" are used almost interchangeably in the popular press, we define "global supply chain management" to mean the management of procurement, sourcing strategy and physical distribution on a global basis. Procurement and sourcing activities constitute *upstream activities* before final products are produced; while physical distribution activities are *downstream activities* that relate more to the marketing activities of the firm.

The costs involved in global supply chain management run very high. Even excluding the cost of materials alone, moving materials and products

– including transportation, warehousing, inventory, customer service/ order entry and administration – is a costly business, with much potential room to improve economic efficiency. Given firms' thin profit margins in a very competitive environment, any cost or waste reductions in the extensive supply chain help improve efficiency, resulting in significant improvements to profitability as well.

3   Managing procurement and sourcing strategy[1]

Introduction

Global supply chain management covers both the procurement and movement of raw materials and components to manufacturing plants and the movement of finished products from plants to customers around the world. It has become imperative for many companies to develop an efficient procurement and sourcing strategy as they attempt to exploit their capabilities in research and development (R&D), manufacturing and marketing – not only on their own, but also with partner suppliers – on a global basis.

An international sourcing strategy is based on the interplay between a company's competitive advantage and the comparative advantages of various countries. "Competitive advantage" refers to an advantage over the competition that a company develops by utilizing not only its own internal resources, but also other external resources available to it. This influences its decision on the activities and technologies on which it should concentrate its investment and managerial resources, relative to competitors in the industry. "Comparative advantage" refers to various locational advantages, such as the availability of inexpensive labor and easy access to port facilities. This influences the company's decision on

---

[1] This chapter is derived primarily from my earlier works, including Masaaki Kotabe and Kristiaan Helsen, *Global Marketing Management,* 9th ed. (Hoboken, NJ: Wiley, 2023), Chapter 15; and Masaaki Kotabe and Janet Y. Murray, "Global Sourcing Strategy: An Evolution in Global Production and Sourcing Rationalization," in Leonidas C. Leonidou, Constantine S. Katsikeas, Saeed Samiee and Bilge Aykol (eds.), *Advances in Global Marketing: A Research Anthology* (New York: Springer, 2018), pp. 365–84. For those interested in more details, please see the above references.

where to source and market, based on the lower cost of labor and other resources in one country relative to another.[2]

Over the last 40 years or so, gradual yet significant changes have taken place in international sourcing strategy. The cost-saving justification for international procurement in the 1980s was gradually supplanted by quality and reliability concerns in the 1990s. In the twenty-first century, the role of international sourcing has become more strategic, managed at the corporate level. It involves a complex mix of insourcing and outsourcing strategies on a global basis. Most of the changes have concerned the way in which business executives think about the scope for international sourcing and exploit various resulting opportunities as a source of competitive advantage for their companies. Naturally, companies that have limited scope for international sourcing are at a disadvantage compared to those that can exploit it to the fullest extent in a globally competitive marketplace. There are eight reasons why companies adopt an international sourcing strategy:

- intense international competition;
- pressure to reduce costs (including the effect of exchange rate fluctuations that affect costs);
- the need for manufacturing flexibility to cope with supply chain disruptions;
- shorter product development cycles as a result of faster technology development;
- stringent quality standards;
- continual changes to product and process technology;
- improvements in information technology (IT); and
- reduced investment in fixed assets to improve profitability.

Toyota's global sourcing operations are one such world-class case. The Japanese carmaker has equipped its operations in the United States, Europe and Southeast Asia with integrated capabilities for manufacturing and marketing automobiles. The company gives executives ample authority to accommodate local circumstances and values without diluting the benefit of integrated global operations. Thus, in the United States, Calty Design Research – a Toyota subsidiary in California – designs the bodies

---

[2]   Bruce Kogut, "Designing Global Strategies: Comparative and Competitive Value-Added Chains," *Sloan Management Review*, 26, Summer 1985: 15–28.

and interiors of new Toyota models, including the Lexus and Camry. Toyota has technical centers in the United States and in Brussels to adapt engine and vehicle specifications to local needs.[3] Toyota's operations that make automobiles in Southeast Asia supply each other with key components to foster increased economies of scale and standardization in those components – gasoline engines in Indonesia, steering components in Malaysia, transmissions in the Philippines and diesel engines in Thailand. In 2003, Toyota also began developing vehicles in Australia and Thailand. These new bases were designed to develop passenger cars and trucks for production and sale in the Asia-Pacific region. The Australian base was engaged mainly in designing cars, whereas the Thailand facility was responsible for testing them.[4] As illustrated by Toyota's decision to close its Australian production base and move it to Thailand by the end of 2017, however, the appreciation of the Australian dollar and the Australian government's unfavorable policy toward inward foreign direct investment became unfavorable factors that made production in and exports from Australia more expensive. Toyota seeks to maintain operational flexibility via global sourcing.[5] Regardless of its manufacturing locations, it endeavors to increase procurement both from local suppliers and from its long-term Japanese suppliers, such as Denso (e.g., for electronic components) and Aisin Seiki (e.g., for engines and drivetrains) – sometimes by asking them to set up operations in Toyota's manufacturing locations.

Historical trends in global sourcing

In recent decades, we have witnessed three distinct trends in global sourcing. The first, which started in the mid-1980s, was primarily based on the decoupling of various aspects of manufacturing activities. Therefore, research was conducted mainly on manufacturing firms. Large manufacturing firms increasingly set up their operations worldwide and started to

[3]   Fumiko Kurosawa and John F. Odgers, "Global Strategy of Design and Development by Japanese Car Makers–From the Perspective of the Resource-Based View," *Association of Japanese Business Studies 1997 Annual Meeting Proceedings*, June 13–15, 1997, pp. 144–46.

[4]   "Toyota Design Breaks from Clay and Foam," *Automotive News Europe*, April 4, 2005, p. 38.

[5]   "Toyota to Exit Australia, 30,000 Jobs Could Go," *Sydney Morning Herald*, www.smh.com.au, February 10, 2014.

buy from suppliers in many countries to exploit best-in-world sources.[6] As a result, supply chains became more global and complex, with manufacturing firms sourcing from suppliers in many countries for raw materials and intermediate and final products in order to reduce labor costs.

A second trend emerged in the early 1990s, when firms started outsourcing their IT departments, which had grown substantially. IT itself was a support function for many manufacturing firms, and many firms thus had little interest in developing new information systems in-house. This IT outsourcing trend spawned the growth of specialist providers such as Accenture and Infosys. Global sourcing mostly involved labor-intensive and standardized programming activities, which could be easily sourced from low-cost locations such as India. The rise of commercial applications for a wide range of firm activities, epitomized in enterprise resource planning systems, also suggested that a marketplace had developed in which independent suppliers could help firms reduce costs and improve operational performance through IT-aided decision-making tools.

A third trend, the offshoring movement, began in the early 2000s. Business process outsourcing has evolved beyond IT services to encompass a range of other services related to accounting, human resource management, finance, sales and after-sales services such as call centers. Between 1992 and 2005, U.S. firms outsourced more than triple the value of services through offshoring.[7]

This third trend in business process outsourcing has generated significant publicity in recent years. Many pundits are concerned that foreign business processes suppliers may be moving up the knowledge chain more quickly than the sourcing firms had expected. This knowledge transfer could undermine sourcing firms' ability to differentiate themselves from their foreign suppliers over time. Indeed, these hollowing-out concerns were previously raised in relation to the outsourcing of manufacturing

---

[6]   James Brian Quinn and Frederick G. Hilmer, "Strategic Outsourcing," *Sloan Management Review*, 35(4), 1994: 43–55.

[7]   Runjuan Liu, Dorothee J. Feils and Barry Scholnick, "Why Are Different Services Outsourced to Different Countries?" *Journal of International Business Studies*, 42, 2011: 558–71.

activities.[8] The successive waves of global sourcing are presented in Table 3.1.

Table 3.1   Trends in global sourcing

Time period	First Trend (Since 1980s)	Second Trend (Since early 1990s)	Third Trend (Since early 2000s)
Type of activity	Manufacturing	Information technology	Business processes
Destinations	China, Central and Eastern Europe, Mexico and others	India, Ireland and others	India, Pakistan, South Africa and others
Types of firms	Manufacturing	Manufacturing, banks and others	Financial services, services more generally
Primary motives	Reduction in labor costs	Access to skilled programmers and cost reductions	Reduction in labor costs and around-the-clock service provision

Procurement: types of sourcing strategy

Sourcing strategy includes a number of basic choices that companies make in deciding how to serve foreign markets. One choice relates to the use of imports, assembly or production within the country to serve a foreign market. Another involves the use of internal or external supplies of components or finished goods.

Sourcing decision-making is multifaceted and entails both contractual and locational implications. From a contractual point of view, the sourc-

---

[8]   Richard A. Bettis, Stephen P. Bradley and Gary Hamel, "Outsourcing and Industrial Decline," *Academy of Management Executive*, 6(1), 1992: 7–16; Masaaki Kotabe, "'Hollowing-out' of U.S. Multinationals and Their Global Competitiveness," *Journal of Business Research*, 19, August 1989: 1–15; Masaaki Kotabe, "Efficiency vs. Effectiveness Orientation of Global Sourcing Strategy: A Comparison of U.S. and Japanese Multinational Companies," *Academy of Management Executive*, 12(4), 1998: 107–19.

ing of major components and products by multinational companies takes place in two ways:

- from parents or foreign subsidiaries on an intrafirm basis, known as "insourcing"; and
- from independent suppliers on a contractual basis, known as "outsourcing."

Similarly, from a locational point of view, multinational companies can procure components and products either:

- domestically (i.e., "domestic sourcing," also known as "onshore sourcing" or just "onshoring"); or
- from abroad (i.e., "offshore sourcing").

Therefore, as shown in Figure 3.1, four possible types of sourcing strategies can be identified.

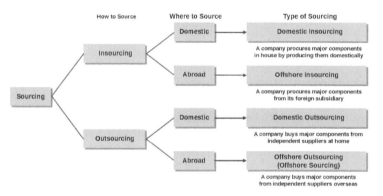

Source: Masaaki Kotabe and Kristiaan Helsen, *Global Marketing Management*, 9th ed (Hoboken, NJ: Wiley, 2023), p. 528.

Figure 3.1   Different sourcing strategies

In developing viable sourcing strategies on a global scale, companies must consider not only the costs of manufacturing and various resources and exchange rate fluctuations, but also the availability of infrastructure (including transportation, communications and energy), industrial and cultural environments, the ease of working with foreign host governments and so on. Furthermore, the complex nature of sourcing strategy on a global scale presents many barriers to successful execution. In particular, logistics, inventory management, distance, nationalism and a lack of working knowledge of foreign business practices, among others, are major operational problems identified by both U.S. and foreign multinational companies when engaging in international sourcing.

Many studies have shown, however, that despite – or perhaps as a result of – those operational problems, *where* to source major components from seems much less important than *how* to source them. Thus, when examining the relationship between sourcing and the competitiveness of multinational companies, it is crucial to distinguish between sourcing on a contractual basis and sourcing on an intrafirm basis, as these different types of sourcing have a different impact on a firm's long-term competitiveness.

Insourcing (or in-house sourcing)

Multinational companies can procure their components in-house within their corporate system around the world. They produce major components at their respective home base and/or at affiliates overseas to be incorporated into products marketed in various parts of the world. Thus, trade takes place between a parent and its subsidiaries abroad and also between foreign subsidiaries across national boundaries. This is often referred to as "insourcing" (or "in-house sourcing"). If such in-house component procurement takes place at home, it essentially constitutes domestic insourcing. If it takes place at a company's foreign subsidiary, it constitutes offshore insourcing. Intrafirm sourcing makes trade statistics more complex to interpret, since part of the international flow of products and components takes place between affiliated companies within the same multinational corporate system, which transcends national boundaries. In 2009, for example, 30 percent of U.S. exports were attributed to U.S. parent companies transferring products and components to affiliates overseas and 48 percent of U.S. imports were accounted for by foreign affiliates exporting to their U.S. parent companies.[9] For both Japan and Britain, intrafirm transactions accounted for approximately 30 percent

---

[9]   Rainer Lanz and Sebastien Miroudot, *Intra-Firm Trade: Patterns, Determinants and Policy Implications*, OECD Trade Policy Papers No. 114 (Paris: OECD Publishing, 2011).

of their total trade flows (exports and imports combined), respectively.[10] This intrafirm trade also reflects the increased role of foreign affiliates of U.S. multinational firms outside the United States.

Outsourcing (contract manufacturing)

In the 1970s, foreign competitors gradually caught up in the productivity race with U.S. companies, which had once commanded a dominant position in international trade. This coincided with U.S. corporate strategic emphasis drifting from manufacturing to finance and marketing. As a result, manufacturing management gradually lost its organizational influence. Production managers' decision-making authority was reduced so that R&D personnel prepared specifications with which production complied and marketing personnel then imposed delivery, inventory and quality conditions. In a sense, production managers gradually took on the role of outside suppliers within their own companies.[11]

Production managers' reduced influence in the organization further led to a belief that manufacturing functions could and should be transferred easily to independent contract manufacturers, depending on the cost differential between in-house and contracted-out production. A company's reliance on domestic suppliers for major components and/or products is basically domestic outsourcing. Furthermore, in order to lower production costs under competitive pressure, U.S. companies increasingly opted to outsource components and finished products from abroad – particularly from China, South Korea, Taiwan and Mexico. Initially, subsidiaries were set up abroad for production purposes (i.e., offshore subsidiary sourcing); but gradually, independent foreign contract manufacturers took over component production for U.S. companies. This latter phenomenon is known by many terms but is usually called "offshore outsourcing" (or, more informally, "offshoring" or "outsourcing"). For example, Apple outsources all of its laptop computers and smartphones to original equipment manufacturers such as Quanta (a Taiwanese

---

[10]   United Nations Center on Transnational Corporations, *Transnational Corporations in World Development: Trends and Perspectives* (New York: United Nations, 1988).

[11]   Stephen S. Cohen and John Zysman, "Why Manufacturing Matters: The Myth of the Post-Industrial Economy," *California Management Review*, 29, Spring 1987: 9–26.

company), Pegatron (a Taiwanese company) and Foxconn (a Taiwanese company operating in China).

Table 3.2   Major reasons for outsourcing

1. Cost reduction	The most obvious and visible benefit relates to the cost savings from outsourcing. Due to differences in wages, the same task can be done in Asian countries at a fraction of the cost in Western countries. The quality of the services provided is high, thereby ensuring that low cost does not necessarily mean low quality.
2. Increased efficiency	Specialized suppliers can develop and deliver products and services more efficiently due to their specialized expertise. This leads to increased productivity and efficiency in the process, thereby contributing to the bottom line of the outsourcing company.
3. Focus on core competencies	Outsourcing business processes allows an outsourcing company to focus on building its brand, investing in R&D and providing higher value-added services.
4. Saving on infrastructure and technology investment	Outsourcing eliminates the need for investment in infrastructure and technology, as suppliers assume responsibility for business processes.
5. Access to skilled expertise	An outsourcing company can rely on suppliers' specialized skills and expertise, which it may not have itself.
6. Time zone advantage	An outsourcing company can rely on suppliers located in different time zones while it is closed for the day. This unique advantage gives an outsourcing company the benefit of round-the-clock business operations.
7. Faster product development and delivery	An outsourcing company can decrease the lead time it takes for its in-house product development to reach the marketplace. It allows the outsourcing company to improve at converting ideas into products and delivering the value-added proposition.

Source: Adapted from Flatworld Solutions, "The Benefits of Outsourcing," www.flatworldsolutions.com.

In recent years, an increasing number of companies have used the internet to develop efficient business-to-business (B2B) procurement (outsourcing) systems on a global scale. On February 25, 2000, General Motors, Ford and DaimlerChrysler made history by jointly forming Covisint (www.covisint.com), probably the largest global online B2B procurement system dedicated to the auto industry. The Big Three were joined by partners Nissan Motor, Renault, Commerce One, Inc. and Oracle Corp. in an effort to provide procurement, supply chain and product development services to the auto industry on a global scale. The auto industry was an early adopter of the B2B procurement business model for a number of marketing-related reasons. First, automakers could develop products with a relatively short lifecycle. Second, they required a fast response time to market. Third, automakers were early adopters of outsourcing, not least due to their efforts to change from a push model to a pull model – that is, to make customized made-to-order marketing feasible.[12] However, by 2004, it became clear that Covisint had not managed to build a relationship of trust between participating automakers and their suppliers, as it had on paper, and it was eventually sold to Compuware Corp. as a messaging data service and portal.[13] Covisint's failure illustrates how difficult it is to manage outsourcing relationships.[14]

Over the past few decades, outsourcing has become a widely used means for U.S. firms in particular to improve their short-term competitive advantage (i.e., financial performance). As outsourcing reduces a firm's fixed investment in its own manufacturing activities, this strategy helps lower the firm's breakeven point and improve its return on investment. First, a lower breakeven point makes a firm less susceptible to fluctuating demand and to a recessionary environment in which sales are low, and thus makes it easier to maintain operational profitability. Second, a high return on investment satisfies a firm's shareholders and helps its stock price appreciate. Indeed, at least in the short run, outsourcing strategy seems like a win-win solution.[15] As a result, many U.S. firms have increased their outsourcing activities. Therefore, the key benefits of outsourcing include cost reduction, increased efficiency, a focus on core

---

[12]   Beverly Beckert, "Engines of Auto Innovation," *Computer-Aided Engineering*, 20, May 2001: S18–S20.

[13]   "Rule of the Road Still Apply to Covisint," *InformationWeek*, February 9, 2004, p. 32.

[14]   Martina Gerst and Raluca Bunduchi, "Shaping IT Standardization in the Automotive Industry – The Role of Power in Driving Portal Standardization," *Electronic Markets*, 15, December 2005: 335–43.

[15]   Masaaki Kotabe and Janet Y. Murray, "Global Sourcing Strategy: An Evolution in Global Production and Sourcing Rationalization," in Leonidas C. Leonidou, Constantine S. Katsikeas, Saeed Samiee and Bilge Aykol (eds.), *Advances in Global Marketing: A Research Anthology* (New York: Springer, 2018), pp. 365–84.

competencies, saving on infrastructure and technology investment, access to skilled expertise, time zone advantage and faster product development and delivery (see Table 3.2).

Concerns over long-term implications

The short- to medium-term benefits of these sourcing strategies seem clear. However, the long-term implications are not so clear. In particular, procurement to independent foreign suppliers (i.e., offshore outsourcing) has received considerable attention, as it not only affects domestic employment and economic structures, but sometimes also raises ethical issues (see Global Viewpoint 3.1). Companies using such strategies have been described pejoratively as "hollow corporations."[16] It is occasionally argued that these companies are increasingly adopting a "designer role" in global competition by offering innovations in product design without investing in manufacturing and process technology. Cultural differences are another key reason why offshore outsourcing deals fail or run into problems in the long run.[17]

Global viewpoint 3.1: Offshore sourcing and sweatshops overseas; an ethical issue

On April 24, 2013, more than 1000 people died and another 2500 were injured when the Rana Plaza garment factory collapsed near Dhaka, Bangladesh. Warnings had been issued the day before about cracks in the walls of the Rana Plaza, but workers were still forced to enter the building on the morning of the collapse.

In Bangladesh, 3.5 million workers in some 5000 garment factories produce goods for export to the global market – principally Europe and North America. The Bangladeshi garment industry generates 80 percent of the country's total export revenue. However, the wealth gener-

---

[16]   "Special Report: The Hollow Corporation," *Business Week*, March 3, 1986, pp. 56–9; Robert Heller, "The Dangers of Deconstruction," *Management Today*, February 1993, pp. 14, 17.

[17]   "Culture Clashes Harm Offshoring," *BusinessWeek.com*, July 17, 2006.

ated by this sector has led to few improvements in the lives of garment workers, 85 percent of whom are women.

North American retailers such as Walmart and GAP are at the head of the list of importers from Bangladesh. In addition, the U.S. government spends about $1.5 billion a year on government uniforms that come from these same factories. These importers favor a model of self-regulation called "corporate social responsibility" (CSR). The flaw with voluntary CSR is that the audits firms pay for are conducted by private companies, not independent entities. They also exclude workers, who are the best monitors of factory conditions. Standing in contrast to the voluntary CSR model is the Bangladesh Accord. Violations of the Bangladesh Accord can be brought before a court of law. In summer 2013, the U.S. House of Representatives passed an amendment to the Defense Authorization Act that would have required military retail stores to source from firms that have signed or adhered to the Bangladesh Accord. However, the amendment did not survive in the House and Senate. This leaves the U.S. government and U.S. taxpayers supporting factories that abuse workers – and sometimes even kill them.

The rapid globalization linking manufacturing companies, investors and consumers around the world has sparked some ethical questions in recent years. Offshore sourcing is the practice of companies manufacturing or contracting out all or part of their production abroad. Outsourcing makes it possible for companies to procure products and components much more cheaply than manufacturing them in their home country. In many cases, labor cost savings are a strong motive for companies to engage in offshore sourcing. For example, leading U.S. footwear company Nike has subcontractors in Taiwan, South Korea and Indonesia; and those Taiwanese and South Korean subcontractors themselves have a number of subcontractors in Indonesia. Thus, Nike collectively runs 12 factories in Indonesia, both directly and indirectly, producing 70 million pairs of Nike sneakers a year. Today, Nike's contractor network involves some 800 000 workers. As with other footwear factories in Asia, work conditions are tough, with workers subjected to mandatory overtime and constant exhaustion. Although these factories may be modern, they are drab and utilitarian, with vast sheds housing row upon row of mostly young women working long hours. The basic daily wage in Indonesia for these workers is a mere $2–3 a day. It costs about $18 to put together a pair of Pegasus running shoes which retails for $75 once shipped to the United States. The conditions are similar in Vietnam, where 35 000 workers producing Nike shoes at five plants put in 12 hours a day to earn $1.60 – less than the $2 or so it costs to buy three meals a day.

Although working conditions at these factories have improved over time at Nike's behest, the company still has a long way to go before it lives up to its stated goal of providing a fair working environment for all its workers. In Indonesia, police and factory managers have a not-so-subtle cozy relationship whereby the police help keep workers under control. Despite its strong political clout, Nike has not challenged the Indonesian government's control over labor. Nike's code of conduct seems to remain vague, despite its intentions.

The linking of a firm's private interests with the larger public good has been referred to as "corporate citizenship." Multinational companies cannot claim ignorance about the workers who produce their products or the conditions under which these people work. Large companies have the resources to investigate those with whom they do business. Ethically speaking, they should set standards that contractors must meet in order to continue their contracts. In recent years, socially responsible investing (SRI) – the practice of making investment decisions on the basis of both financial and social performance – has grown in prominence. The SRI movement has evolved into a $1.185 trillion business, accounting for about $1 in every $10 invested.

An exhaustive academic review of 167 studies over the past 35 years concluded that there is in fact a positive link between companies' social and financial performance – albeit only a weak one. But this does not mean that it is not worth the effort because companies will benefit a lot from building a better brand reputation, making decisions that are better for business in the long term, being more attractive to potential and existing employees and so on.

Source: R. Bruce Hutton, Louis D'Antonio, and Tommi Johnsen, "Socially Responsible Investing: Growing Issues and New Opportunities," *Business and Society*, 37, September 1998: 281-305; "Labor Standards Clash with Global Reality," *New York Times*, April 24, 2001; "Cops of the Global Village," *Fortune*, June 27, 2005, pp. 158-66; "The Next Question," *Economist*, January 19, 2008, Special Section, pp. 8-10; "Bangladesh Factory Collapse Toll Passes 1,000," *BBC News*, www.bbc.com, May 10, 2013; "How Your Tax Dollars are Funding Overseas Sweatshops," www.thenation.com, January 7, 2014; and "Sweatshops in Bangladesh," *War on Want*, waronwant.org, March 8, 2019.

The cost versus quality issue

Even Covisint, the global B2B procurement business founded by the Big Three automakers, discussed earlier, was unable to generate the results that its participants had initially expected. Typical B2B procurement systems, including Covisint, have tended to rely on auctions that emphasize the lowest bids on a global basis. This internet-era emphasis on low cost resembles the cost emphasis of the 1960s and 1970s, which ignored the importance of quality, technological superiority, delivery and other non-cost aspects of competitive advantage. In fact, to achieve superior product development when partnering with external suppliers, automakers should emphasize the importance of technical collaborations, such as product design, as well as building trust in supplier-buyer relationships.[18]

Supply disruptions

For global supply chains to operate efficiently, the market environment – and particularly the logistics environment – must be relatively stable. First, modes of logistics – including air freight, ocean shipping and inland transportation – must be functioning properly, without interruptions such as those caused by strikes and various types of natural disasters (e.g., hurricanes, earthquakes, volcanic eruptions and pandemics). Second, rampant exchange rate fluctuations can wreak havoc on the pricing/costing of materials shipped across national boundaries. This is all the more so the more globally dispersed the supply chain is,

---

[18]   Masaaki Kotabe, Xavier Martin and Hiroshi Domoto, "Gaining from Vertical Relationships: Knowledge Transfer, Relationship Duration, and Supplier Performance Improvement in the U.S. and Japanese Automobile Industries," *Strategic Management Journal*, 24, March 2003: 293–316.

simply because exchange rate fluctuations can make it very difficult for the sourcing company to keep track of ever-changing cost environments. Sometimes, it makes you wonder why companies like Toyota conduct procurement activities in geographical proximity rather than in a globally dispersed fashion. Third, political disruptions cannot be ignored. In recent years, the U.S.-China trade war and Russia's invasion of Ukraine have caused severe disruptions to what would otherwise have been smooth international trade.

In fact, companies like Toyota started addressing the importance of not only collaborating with external suppliers, but also knowing and dealing with supply disruptions that might occur along a vast chain of multiple layers of suppliers on a global basis. Indeed, when the COVID-19 pandemic caused a global supply shortage of semiconductor chips for automobile production in 2021, most automakers – including GM, Ford, Daimler, BMW and Renault – had to slash production by as much as 50 percent.[19] However, Toyota's production was virtually unscathed, thanks to its REinforce Supply Chain Under Emergency (RESCUE) program. RESCUE makes Toyota's procurement network "visible" from the first all the way to tenth suppliers on a global basis, classifies components into one of eight categories according to differences in supply disruption risk, and assesses high-risk components together with suppliers for alternative procurement methods and a stable supply path.[20] Such capabilities in managing buyer-supplier relationships are becoming all the more important in maintaining market competitiveness in increasingly volatile, uncertain, complex and ambiguous global environments.

Outsourcing of service activities

In 2022, the United States was the leading exporter and importer of commercial services, providing $929 billion worth of services to the rest of the world and receiving $697 billion worth of services from

---

[19]   "How Toyota Kept Making Cars when the Chips were Down," *Fortune*, www.fortune.com, August 2, 2021.

[20]   Takahiro Fujimoto, Mihail Marinov, Yumi Kato and Shumpei Iwao, "Strengthening Purchasing and Supply Chain Management at Toyota, A Working Paper, University of Tokyo, June 2019; "トヨタ、代替生産の追求で描く欠品ゼロ - 在庫は増やさず ("Toyota in Pursuit of Zero Shortage – without an Increase in Inventory"), www.Business.nikkei.com, July 31, 2020.

abroad.[21] Furthermore, according to a recent Organisation for Economic Co-operation and Development (OECD) estimate, trade of services conducted across national boundaries on an intrafirm basis (i.e., between parent companies and their subsidiaries) in the United Sates has also increased. The share of intrafirm exports in total private service exports in the United States increased by six percentage points from 20 percent in 1992 to 26 percent in 2008 (more recent statistics were not available). The respective increase in the share of intrafirm imports was by nine percentage points, from 13 percent to 22 percent.[22] Clearly, U.S. companies have expanded their service procurement activities on a global basis in the same way as they procured components and finished products.[23] In 2021, according to A.T. Kearney's Global Services Location Index, India and China were the top two most attractive offshoring locations, with Malaysia, Indonesia and Brazil rounding out the top five.[24]

As discussed, firms have the ability and opportunity to procure components/finished goods that have proprietary technology on a global basis. This logic equally applies to service activities. The technological revolution in data processing and telecommunications (e.g., transborder data flow, telematics) has both made the global tradability of some services possible and facilitated such transactions from an economic perspective. Furthermore, because the production and consumption of some services need not take place at the same location or at the same time, global sourcing may be a viable strategy.

Thanks to the development of the internet and e-commerce, certain service activities are increasingly outsourced to independent service suppliers. The internet has also accelerated an increase in the number of e-workers. This net-savvy, highly flexible corps can undertake much or all of their work at home or in small groups close to home, regardless of location. International e-workers (commonly known as digital nomads) can also operate in locations far from corporate headquarters. They are

---

[21]   "International Services (Expanded Detail)," www.bea.org.
[22]   Rainer Lanz and Sebastien Miroudot, *Intra-Firm Trade: Patterns, Determinants and Policy Implications*, OECD Trade Policy Papers, No. 114 (OECD Publishing, 2011), https://doi.org/10.1787/5kg9p39lrwnn-en.
[23]   "Global Outsourcing to Grow 8% in 2008," *BusinessWeek.com*, January 10, 2008.
[24]   "Toward a Global Network of Digital Hubs: The 2021 Kearney Global Services Location Index," A.T. Kearney Consulting, www.atkearney.com.

part of the growth in *intellectual outsourcing*. Such e-workers can write software in India for a phone company in Finland, provide architectural services in Ireland for a building in Spain and do accounting work in Hong Kong for an insurance company in Vancouver, Canada. The globalization of services through the internet is likely to expand considerably in the future.

Bengaluru is one key example. The region has been described as India's Silicon Valley. Bengaluru has rapidly evolved to become an offshore programming center. Many U.S. companies have started outsourcing their software development to companies in Bengaluru. Established software vendors – including IBM, Microsoft, Oracle and SAP – employ Indian talent no longer just to write software code but also to help design and develop commercial offerings that are higher up in the software design food chain. Increasingly, Indian software entrepreneurs want to put their own companies' brand names on products, at home and abroad, by capitalizing on India's highly educated, low-cost workforce to build and sell software for everything from back-office programs to customer-facing applications.[25] According to the National Association of Software and Services Companies in India (NASSCOM), IT services were forecast to grow by 4.8 percent in 2019. India's computer software/services and IT-enabled services sector also grew by 3.83 percent to $111 billion from 2016 to 2017.[26] Microsoft has 11 research laboratories located around the globe – including in China, India, Egypt, Israel, Germany and the United Kingdom, as well as in the United States – with the goal of investing in its future by focusing on technologies and technology trends within a five- to ten-year timeframe. For example, Microsoft Research Asia, founded in 1998 in Beijing, has already produced many research results that have been transferred to Microsoft products, including Windows and Office software.

The outsourcing of service activities has been widely quoted in the popular press as a means to reduce costs and tighten corporate focus by

---

[25]   "India's Next Step," *InformationWeek*, August 8, 2005, pp. 34–9.
[26]   "India's Software, ITeS exports clocks at $111 Billion," *The Economic Times*, economictimes.com, January 25, 2018.

concentrating on the firm's core activities. However, outsourcing may also serve as a means of:

- reducing time to implement internal processes;
- sharing risk in an increasingly uncertain business environment;
- improving customer service;
- accessing better expertise that is not available in-house;
- cutting headcount; and
- instilling a sense of competition, especially when departments within firms develop a perceptible level of inertia.[27]

Despite its advantages and attractiveness to businesses, offshore outsourcing can have an adverse impact on some other stakeholders – namely, the workforce in the home country. See Global Viewpoint 3.2 for some broad issues relating to the offshoring of services.

Global viewpoint 3.2: Trends and potential disruption in service offshoring

For years, India has been the number one choice for U.S. companies seeking to offshore service jobs. India's outsourcing sector grew to about $118 billion in 2017. India has substantial advantages in offshoring, including plenty of English speakers to staff call centers and enough tech talent to run remote data-processing and computer support centers, who work at a discount of around 60 percent compared to U.S. workers. According to NASSCOM, India's share of the global outsourcing market has increased by more than 50 percent since 2009. India still stands out for its customer service and efficiency. Today, customers are looking not only for cost-effective solutions for their outsourced business, but also for skilled staff, enhanced productivity, service quality and business process excellence. India – with its large and highly skilled population – remains preferred for both back-end and front-end outsourcing.

In recent years, the United States has outsourced tens of thousands of

---

[27]   Maneesh Chandra, "Global Sourcing of Services: A Theory Development and Empirical Investigation," Ph.D. dissertation, University of Texas at Austin, 1999.

jobs to India, ranging from technology support to Wall Street research. The argument made by corporate executives, politicians and academics was that there was no choice. Especially in light of globalization, it is critical to tap the lower costs and unique skills of labor abroad to remain competitive. This trend has raised fears in the United States that the U.S. economy may be permanently losing certain jobs and job categories. This could lead to a hollowing out of the middle class and downward pressure on wages. In a 2004 paper, Nobel Prize-winning economist Paul Samuelson stated that "the economic effect of outsourcing is similar to allowing mass immigration of workers willing to compete for service jobs at extremely low wages."

Despite its overall economic gains, offshoring is also redistributive, with affected workers facing possible job losses and wage pressures. McKinsey and Co. conducted a study to estimate the redistribution effect. Both the theory and the evidence provide only partial answers. The McKinsey study estimates that for every dollar of U.S. services activity that is offshored, there is a global gain of $1.47, suggesting a net gain of 47 cents. India captures 33 cents of the total, leaving the United States with the remaining $1.14. How is this $1.14 distributed? "Reemployed" workers get 47 cents (a substantial reduction); additional exports account for a relatively modest 5 cents; and shareholders and consumers of the firms doing the offshoring gain the other 62 cents. U.S. shareholders and consumers win, while U.S. workers lose.

Paradoxically, recent development in robotics may help reduce U.S. firms' reliance on service offshoring and bring back "home-shoring." Just as robotics has been transforming manufacturing and process industries in recent years, robotic process automation (RPA) has begun to ripple through the U.S. service economy. After all, back-office employees spend roughly one-quarter of their time on repetitive, rules-based tasks – precisely those which are easiest to automate. RPA software processes operations three times faster than the average human around the clock and without errors. On average, a software robot (in essence, an RPA license) costs one-third as much as an offshore employee and one-fifth as much as onshore staff. As a result, RPA can produce savings of between 25 and 50 percent in select back-office processes at home. However, the economic benefit of increased "home-shoring" may continue to benefit U.S. shareholders and consumers at the expense of U.S. workers being further displaced by automation.

Significant players in RPA include Blue Prism (which founded the field), Automation Anywhere and New York-based WorkFusion – a privately held company that grew out of research at the Massachusetts Institute of Technology's Computer Science and Artificial Intelligence Lab pairing people with machine-learning algorithms. Some major IT companies, such as IBM and Xerox, have also established RPA business units recently.

Could this mean the beginning of the end of India's dominance in the global outsourcing market? Indian service providers are not sitting still. They are increasingly using standardized interfaces and processes across multiple customers – with varying degrees of automation – to quickly deliver outcomes at any scale. With the advent of cloud computing, these service providers are looking at a more service-oriented approach to services, known as business-process-as-a-service (BPaaS). Rather than using each customer's company-specific processes, BPaaS employs a standardized platform based in the cloud. The standardized offerings of BPaaS are particularly well suited to smaller service providers, which have neither the volume to enter into large contracts nor the need to outsource more than a few relatively simple processes from the cloud. Given the minimal fixed costs required to accommodate additional customers, BPaaS could usher in a new generation of nimble outsourcing companies in India.

Source: Lael Brainard and Robert E. Litan, "'Offshoring' Service Jobs: Bane or Boon – and What to Do?," *Brookings Institution Policy Brief*, April 2004; John Helyar, "Outsourcing: A Passage out of India," *Bloomberg Businessweek*, March 15, 2012; "Outsourcing: 6 Reasons Why India is Preferred for Outsourcing," *Resourcifi*, www.resourcifi.com, July 12, 2018; "Outsourcing to India: A Global Need for Outsourcing," Backoffice Pro, www.backofficepro.com.

In the case of service companies, the distinction between core and supplementary services is necessary for strategy development. Core services are the necessary outputs of an organization that consumers are looking for; while supplementary services are either indispensable to execution of the core service or available only to improve the overall quality of the core service bundle. Using the example of the healthcare industry, the core service is providing patients with good-quality medical care. Supplementary services may include filing insurance claims, arranging accommodation for family members (especially overseas patients), handling out-of-hours emergency calls and so on. The same phenomenon arises in the computer software industry. When industry giant Microsoft needed help supporting new users of Windows operating software, it utilized outsourcing with Boston-based Keane, Inc. to set up a help desk with 350 support personnel.

Core services may gradually become a "commodity" and lose their differential advantage *vis-à-vis* competitors as competition intensifies over time. Subsequently, a service provider may increase its reliance on supplementary services to maintain and/or enhance competitive advantage. "After all, if a firm cannot do a decent job on the core elements, it is eventually going to go out of business."[28] In other words, a service firm exists in order to provide good-quality core services to its customers; however, in some instances, it simply cannot rely solely on core services to stay competitive. We can expect that core services are usually performed by the service firm itself, regardless of their characteristics. On the other hand, although supplementary services are provided to augment the core services for competitive advantage, their unique characteristics may influence "how" and "where" they are sourced.[29]

It is important to acknowledge that U.S. consumers exhibit a country of service origin preference. When receiving an offshore service, they consider communication, security and reliability as the most important service quality attributes.[30] Therefore, it is imperative for U.S. companies (and for other companies across the world considering offshoring their services) to consider and be aware of consumer attitudes and perceptions about the countries that are considered attractive for offshoring. Countries with the highest skilled labor, lowest cost or geographical prox-

---

[28]   Christopher H. Lovelock, "Adding Value to Core Products with Supplementary Services," in Christopher H. Lovelock (ed.), *Services Marketing*, 3rd ed. (Englewood Cliffs, NJ: Prentice-Hall, 1996).

[29]   Terry Clark, Daniel Rajaratnam and Timothy Smith, "Toward a Theory of International Services: Marketing Intangibles in a World of Nations," *Journal of International Marketing*, 4(2), 1996: 9–28; Janet Y. Murray and Masaaki Kotabe, "Sourcing Strategies of U.S. Service Companies: A Modified Transaction-Cost Analysis," *Strategic Management Journal*, 20, September 1999: 791–809.

[30]   Shawn T. Thelen, Earl D. Honeycutt, Jr. and Thomas P. Murphy, "Services Offshoring: Does Perceived Service Quality Affect Country-of-Service Origin Preference?" *Managing Service Quality*, 20(3), 2010: 196–212.

imity to the home country may not necessarily be preferred for service offshoring.

The bottom line is that the quality of the service package that customers experience helps service companies differentiate themselves from the competition. One important aspect of quality is the reliablity of the product or service's attributes. As in manufacturing, service companies that choose to differentiate themselves based on reliability must consistently maintain it; otherwise, they will undermine their strategic position by damaging the reputation of their brand. There is empirical evidence that outsourcing of some service activities for the sake of economic efficiency tends to result in less reliable service offerings.[31] The same concerns about the advantages and disadvantages of outsourcing in the manufacturing industry would also appear to apply in the services industry.

Summary

Increased global sourcing of manufacturing and service activities to independent suppliers has been a prominent part of the restructuring of firms' supply chains since the 1980s. Academics and consulting companies have advocated global sourcing as a key driver of superior corporate strategy which has a direct impact on market performance, including market share, product quality, customer satisfaction and brand loyalty, among others.

In this chapter, we first discussed the nature of global sourcing strategy in the manufacturing sector as it has evolved in response to the changing climate since the 1980s. Sourcing strategies can be categorized in terms of ownership (how to source) and location (where to source). Firms' decisions on the types of sourcing depend on a complex interplay between factors such as cost, operational and quality control, flexibility, strategic goals and so on. Most of the discussion on global sourcing tends to focus on short- to medium-term benefits. We also explored

---

[31]   C. M. Hsieh, Sergio G. Lazzarini and Jack A. Nickerson, "Outsourcing and the Variability of Product Performance: Data from International Courier Services," *Academy of Management Proceedings*, 2002: G1–G6.

the long-term implications of various sourcing strategies, particularly outsourcing strategies, as they have become popular as a way to reduce long-term fixed investment needs and to improve firms' bottom line (i.e., profitability). Some caveats – such as the cost and quality issue and supply disruptions – were examined. Finally, although offshore outsourcing strategies started in the manufacturing sector, firms in the service sector have also begun to experience the benefits (and costs) of outsourcing service activities in recent decades, particularly as a result of IT advancements.

4 Global sourcing strategy and performance[1]

Introduction

We focus on the global supply chain in this book as it adds many complexities that do not apply to domestic sourcing strategy. When developing viable global sourcing strategies, firms must also consider the availability of infrastructure (including transportation, communications and energy), industrial and cultural environments, the ease of working with foreign host governments and other factors, in addition to manufacturing and delivery costs, the costs of various resources and exchange rate fluctuations. Furthermore, the complexity of global sourcing strategy creates many barriers to its successful execution. For example, logistics, inventory management, distance, nationalism and a lack of working knowledge about foreign business practices, among other things, are major operational problems faced by both U.S. and foreign multinational firms engaging in global sourcing.

Intuitive arguments, like focusing on "core competency"[2] and "strategic sourcing," are often made to legitimize the trend toward more global outsourcing. Simply stated, the firm should focus on what it can do best

---

[1] This chapter is primarily derived from my earlier works, including Masaaki Kotabe and Janet Y. Murray, "Global Sourcing Strategy: An Evolution in Global Production and Sourcing Rationalization," in Leonidas C. Leonidou, Constantine S. Katsikeas, Saeed Samiee and Bilge Aykol (eds.), *Advances in Global Marketing: A Research Anthology* (New York: Springer, 2018), pp. 365–84; and Masaaki Kotabe, Michael J. Mol, Janet Y. Murray and Ronaldo Parente, "The Limits to Outsourcing: Beware of the Consequences for Market Success," *World Financial Review*, January-February 2013: 11–14.

[2] The core competency argument was popularized in C.K. Prahalad and Gary Hamel, "The Core Competence of the Corporation", *Harvard Business Review*, 68(3), 1990: 79–91.

for competitive advantage and outsource peripheral activities to outside contractors, just as Apple focuses on product design and outsources production of iPhones to Taiwan's Foxconn, which manufactures in China.

We first discuss recent trends in global supply chain management. Then, we highlight the advantages and disadvantages of global sourcing by providing a list of intuitive arguments for each. We then attempt to explain global sourcing levels and how these relate to performance.

Global sourcing strategy and performance

Since one of the firm's main concerns is delivering value to the end user, efficient supply chains are perhaps the greatest imperative for the marketing function.[3] An effective and efficient supply contributes to marketing's domain in providing value and satisfaction to customers, which ultimately improves the firm's performance. Likewise, global sourcing is broadly considered to improve performance, particularly cost effectiveness.[4] Firms in developed countries are often confronted with expensive labor costs, compared to the value that is added to their products. At the other extreme, some global sourcing may be driven by knowledge concerns. Some inputs – such as digital image sensors and certain technical expertise – may be available only in certain other countries, thus making global sourcing not a choice but a necessity. As for the sourcing of many raw materials, domestic sourcing is not always an option since many raw materials are unavailable domestically. Certain intermediate products tend to be sourced from locations near the source of raw materials. Another argument in favor of global sourcing is that it allows a firm to produce closer to its customer markets, thereby increasing access to them and obtaining critical market knowledge for product development. For instance, Japanese manufacturing firms have replicated their supply chains in North America and Europe over time in order to operate

---

3   Irina V. Kozlenkova, G. Tomas M. Hult, Donald J. Lund, Jeannette A. Mena and Pinar Kekec, "The Role of Marketing Channels in Supply Chain Management," *Journal of Retailing*, 91(4), 2015: 586–609.

4   Robert Trent and Robert Monczka, "International Purchasing and Global Sourcing – What Are the Differences?" *Journal of Supply Chain Management*, 39(4), 2003: 26–37.

closer to these markets. Their production and sourcing experience in these regions has also enabled them to improve their product offerings. Another reason to opt for global sourcing is that demand from various regions can be pooled, thus achieving maximum scale and bargaining power through single sourcing from a foreign supplier.

On the other hand, there are disadvantages associated with global sourcing. One major problem is cultural differences between buyers and their foreign suppliers.[5] Indeed, differences such as institutional and language problems may negatively affect these relationships. This raises other issues related to the long-term sustainability of firms' core competencies – in particular, when firms increase their reliance on independent suppliers through outsourcing.[6] There are two opposing views of the long-term implications of outsourcing. One school of thought argues that many successful firms have developed a dynamic network capability through increasing cross-border joint ventures, licensing and subcontracting activities.[7] This flexible network system, also known as "supply chain alliances," allows each participant to pursue its own unique competence. Each network participant complements rather than competes against the others for the common goals. The other school of thought argues that while firms may gain short-term advantages, negative consequences can develop over time. As firms become more dependent on their independent suppliers, they may be unable to keep abreast of constantly evolving design and engineering technologies without engaging themselves in these developmental activities.[8] As a result, firms encounter the inherent difficulty of sustaining their long-term competitive advantage. In other words, over time, firms' technical expertise and capability surplus *vis-à-vis* foreign suppliers may diminish to the point that their added

5   Dina Ribbink and Curtis M. Grimm, "The Impact of Cultural Differences on Buyer–Supplier Negotiations: An Experimental Study," *Journal of Operations Management*, 32(3), 2014: 114–26.
6   For a more extensive discussion of outsourcing and core competencies, see Michael J. Mol, *Outsourcing: Design, Process, and Performance* (Cambridge: Cambridge University Press, 2007).
7   Raymond E. Miles and Charles C. Snow, "Organizations: New Concepts for New Firms," *California Management Review*, 28, Spring 1986: 62–73.
8   Masaaki Kotabe, *Global Sourcing Strategy: R&D, Manufacturing, and Marketing Interfaces* (New York: Quorum Books, 1992); Masaaki Kotabe, "Efficiency vs. Effectiveness Orientation of Global Sourcing Strategy: A Comparison of U.S. and Japanese Multinational Companies," *Academy of Management Executive*, 12, November 1998: 107–19.

value is limited and they become more like trading companies. Thus, based on the arguments for and against outsourcing, we need to synthesize our thinking on outsourcing and performance. A summary of these opposing arguments is presented in Table 4.1.

The primary objective of a firm's global sourcing strategy is to develop a cost-efficient delivery mechanism which helps increase the market performance of its international marketing strategy. An effective and efficient global sourcing strategy helps decrease selling prices through cost reduction, improve delivery time, secure the right inventory and ultimately increase international market performance. The effect of global sourcing strategy on international market performance may include product differentiation, consumer confidence, brand equity and corporate reputation, among other things.[9]

In today's hypercompetitive markets, firms must reduce costs and achieve high product quality while simultaneously responding quickly to global market turbulence.[10] Thus, developing a new supply chain system that can achieve both high-quality production standards and low-cost operations has become of utmost importance. Indeed, marketing transactions encompass both the buying (i.e., supply chain) and selling (i.e., market selection) aspects of the exchange process. Although marketing organizations are examined mainly in their roles as sellers rather than as buyers, the buying aspect (i.e., supply chain issues) of the exchange process should not be ignored.[11] The boundary-spanning marketing organization that must be developed and maintained depends on how well the marketing activities, customer value-creating business processes, networks and stakeholder focus are molded together to form an integrated organization. The primary objective of global sourcing strategy is to develop a task-effective delivery mechanism for customer satisfaction.[12] Since

[9]   Masaaki Kotabe, Michael J. Mol, Janet Y. Murray and Ronaldo Parente, "Outsourcing and its Implications for Market Success: Negative Curvilinearity, Firm Resources, and Competition," *Journal of the Academy of Marketing Science*, 40, March 2012: 329–46.

[10]   Richard D'Aveni, *Hypercompetition: Managing the Dynamics of Strategic Management* (New York: Free Press, 1994).

[11]   Phillip Kotler and Sidney J. Levy, "Buying is Marketing, Too," *Journal of Marketing*, 37(1), 1973: 54–9.

[12]   G. Thomas Hult, "Toward a Theory of the Boundary-Spanning Marketing Organization and Insights from 31 Organization Theories," *Journal of the Academy of Marketing Science,* 39, 2011: 509–36.

Table 4.1   Arguments for and against outsourcing

The Case *For* Outsourcing	The Case *Against* Outsourcing
Strategic focus/reduction of assets: Through outsourcing activities, a firm can reduce its asset investment in manufacturing and related areas. Since more or less similar absolute profit levels can be obtained with lower fixed investments, the firm's return on investment position improves. Furthermore, outsourcing can permit the management of a firm to focus on its core competencies, instead of having to possess and update a wide range of competencies.	**Interfaces/economies of scope:** Firms may benefit from internalizing production through scope economies. If there are important interfaces among R&D, manufacturing and marketing activities, decoupling them into separate activities performed by different suppliers will generate less than optimal results. Manufacturing firms, in their outsourcing decisions, need to reflect on the hidden cost of losing interfaces among these activities.
Strategic flexibility: Outsourcing may increase the firm's strategic flexibility. By using outsourcing, it is much easier to switch from one supplier to another. If an external shock occurs, firms can react quickly by simply increasing or decreasing the volumes obtained from external suppliers. If the same item were produced in-house, firms would incur not only high restructuring costs but also a much longer response time to external events.	**Hollowing out:** Firms that outsource activities excessively are hollowing out their competitive base. Once intertwined activities have been outsourced, it becomes difficult to differentiate a firm's products on the basis of these activities. Furthermore, a firm can lose bargaining power *vis-à-vis* its suppliers because its suppliers' capabilities may increase relative to those of the firm.
Avoiding bureaucratic costs: Internal production is associated with rising production costs, due to the lack of a price mechanism and economic incentives inside a firm. As a result, firm efficiency will suffer.	**Opportunistic behavior:** External suppliers may behave opportunistically as their incentive structure may diverge considerably from that of the outsourcing firm. Opportunistic behavior allows a supplier to extract more rents from the relationship than it would normally do – for example, by supplying lower than agreed-upon product quality or withholding information on changes in production costs.

The Case *For* Outsourcing	The Case *Against* Outsourcing
Relational rent: In recent years, many researchers have argued that certain relationships with external suppliers can help firms create a unique competitive advantage aided by their suppliers' knowledge. By outsourcing items based on idiosyncratic and valuable relationships with suppliers, firms may be able to innovate, learn and reduce transaction costs.	**Rising transaction and coordination costs:** Excessive outsourcing may lead to high coordination costs. Firms have limited capacity to work with outside suppliers as partners and therefore must prioritize those outside partners. If they simultaneously invested time and attention in all outside suppliers, this would result in very high coordination costs.
	Limited learning and innovation: A form of learning that is deemed especially important for obtaining tacit knowledge is "learning by doing." The supplier may acquire tacit knowledge by performing the activity; consequently, the outsourcing firm cannot appropriate all benefits. Appropriation of innovation and rents is always a problem in buyer-supplier relationships because both parties will try to obtain as many private benefits as possible. Furthermore, it may become more difficult to innovate, due to the different incentives available and the subsequent lack of interfaces between firms.

Source: Adapted from Masaaki Kotabe, Michael J. Mol, and Janet Y. Murray, "Global Sourcing Strategy," in Masaaki Kotabe and Kristiaan Helsen, eds., *The SAGE Handbook of International Marketing* (London: Sage Publications, 2009), pp. 288–302.

firms must deal with a drastically shortened lifecycle for most products in an era of global competition, it is not advisable to adopt a polycentric, country-by-country approach to international business. If firms that have developed a new product adopt a country-by-country approach to foreign market entry, over time a globally oriented competitor will likely overcome their initial competitive advantages by blanketing the world market with similar products in a shorter time interval. Therefore, it is important for firms to continuously develop and acquire capabilities that will help them generate a sustainable competitive advantage over competitors. Increasingly, using outsourcing to source globally has become a critical strategic decision that is affected by the capabilities needed to compete.

"It's no longer a company's ownership of capabilities that matters but rather its ability to control and make the most of critical capabilities, whether or not they reside on the company's balance sheet."[13]

Globally acclaimed management guru Jay Barney has emphasized that firms possess sustained competitive advantage both when they adopt a strategy that is "not simultaneously being implemented by any current or potential competitors *and* when these other firms are unable to duplicate the benefits of this strategy."[14] However, simply having product innovations does not guarantee that firms will enjoy a sustainable competitive advantage. Rather, firms should be able to complement their product innovations with powerful manufacturing and marketing capabilities. This is mainly because in today's highly competitive market, protecting proprietary technology through legal means has become ineffective as new product innovations are easily reverse engineered, improved upon and invented around by competing firms without violating patents and other proprietary protections.[15] Production sharing facilitates technology diffusion through traditional and non-traditional channels among competitors. Thus, the value of owning technological know-how has reduced drastically as the inventing company's temporary monopoly over its technological know-how has become transient.

In a highly competitive environment, many manufacturers either produce in lower-cost locations or outsource components and finished products from lower-cost producers on a contractual original equipment manufacturer (OEM) basis. However, firms increasingly outsource to gain access to suppliers' capabilities.[16] The ultimate objective of global sourcing strategy is for the firm to exploit both its own and its suppliers' competitive advantages and the locational advantages of various countries to better serve customers on a global basis. Indeed, when rivals such as UPS and

---

[13]   Mark Gottfredson, Rudy Puryear and Stephen Phillips, "Strategic Sourcing – From Periphery to the Core," *Harvard Business Review*, 83(2), 2005: 132–39.

[14]   Jay Barney, "Firm Resources and Sustained Competitive Advantage," *Journal of Management*, 17(1), 1991: 99–120.

[15]   Richard C. Levin, Alvin K. Klevorick, Richard Nelson and Sidney Winter, "Appropriating the Returns from Industrial Research and Development," *Brookings Papers on Economic Activity*, 3, 1987: 783–831.

[16]   Jay B. Barney, "How a Firm's Capabilities Affect Boundary Decisions," *Sloan Management Review*, 40(3), 1999: 37–145.

FedEx clash, it is not merely their individual capabilities, but rather the collective capabilities of their respective supply chains which determine the outcome.[17]

Although firms have embraced global sourcing of goods and services, they have experienced mixed results. In one study, about 50 percent of firms in the sample reported that their outsourcing programs did not live up to expectations.[18] Only 10 percent were highly satisfied with the cost savings and just 6 percent were highly satisfied with their offshore outsourcing overall. Other researchers have even suggested that outsourcing may not be related to performance.[19] Due to inconclusive performance outcomes, practitioners have started to question whether universally prescribing global outsourcing is the right approach.

These ambiguous observations, as well as academic arguments about the benefits of outsourcing, raise some serious managerial questions. Outsourcing may be an effective way to cut costs in the short run, but do you know how it affects the success of your firm in the marketplace over the long term? In this chapter, we share some insights and hope to provide you with guidance on how to achieve a balanced outsourcing strategy.

Outsourcing helps reduce fixed investment in in-house manufacturing facilities and thus lower the breakeven point, making a company less susceptible to recessionary sales declines and potentially helping to boost its return on investment (ROI). Thus, if the performance of corporate executives is evaluated based on their contribution to the company's ROI, they tend to have an incentive to increase outsourcing – especially in a business environment where pressures for cost reduction are everywhere. This

---

[17]   G. Tomas M. Hult, David J. Ketchen and Mathias Arrfelt, "Strategic Supply Chain Management: Improving Performance through a Culture of Competitiveness and Knowledge Development," *Strategic Management Journal*, 28, 2007: 1035–52.

[18]   Mark Gottfredson, Rudy Puryear and Stephen Phillips, "Strategic Sourcing – From Periphery to the Core," *Harvard Business Review*, 83(2), 2005: 132–39.

[19]   Michael J. Leiblein, Jeffrey J. Reuer and Frédéric Dalsace, "Do Make or Buy Decisions Matter? The Influence of Organizational Governance on Technological Performance," *Strategic Management Journal*, 23(9), 2002: 817–33.

financial logic has appealed, in particular, to U.S. corporate executives, who tend to be evaluated on relatively short-term results.

At the other end of the value chain, marketers and top executives may not have considered the marketing consequences of outsourcing strategy to the same extent. Can an outsourcing strategy help sustain your firm's competitiveness in the marketplace in the long run? Although the marketing performance impact of various strategic issues – such as market structure, brand equity, market share and competitive strategies – has been widely studied, the outsourcing-marketing performance nexus has eluded executives' attention.

But we have strong reasons to believe that it matters and should be considered alongside these other issues. A series of studies[20] that we have conducted point to the fact that although firms may be able to improve their profitability and market share through outsourcing, this is true only up to a point, beyond which market share decreases because of further outsourcing. Furthermore, we have found large-scale outsourcing to be a suitable strategy only for firms that have weak internal resources and face intense competition in the marketplace.

Before we explore the practical implications of our research, let us consider three historical cases from the personal computer (PC) industry. First, Michael Dell established Dell Computer in the 1980s because he had spotted a burgeoning market for IBM-compatible PCs in the United States. After his immediate success at home, the company began export-

---

[20] Masaaki Kotabe, Michael J. Mol, Janet Y. Murray and Ronaldo Parente, "Outsourcing and its Implications for Market Success: Negative Curvilinearity, Firm Resources, and Competition," *Journal of the Academy of Marketing Science*, 40(2), 2012: 329–46; Michael J. Mol and Masaaki Kotabe, "Overcoming Inertia: Drivers of the Outsourcing Process," *Long Range Planning*, 44, May 2011: 160–78; Masaaki Kotabe and Michal J. Mol, "Outsourcing and Financial Performance: A Negative Curvilinear Relationship," *Journal of Purchasing and Supply Management*, 15(4), 2009: 205–13; Masaaki Kotabe, Michael J. Mol and Sonia Ketkar, "An Evolutionary Stage Model of Outsourcing and Competence Destruction: A Triad Comparison of the Consumer Electronics Industry," *Management International Review*, 48(1) 2008: 65–93; and Masaaki Kotabe, Michael J. Mol and Janet Y. Murray, "Outsourcing, Performance, and the Role of E-Commerce: A Dynamic Perspective," *Industrial Marketing Management*, 37(1), 2008: 37–45.

ing Dell PCs to Europe and Japan, followed by foreign production and subsequent outsourcing of more of its production to Quanta, a leading Taiwanese computer contract manufacturer, just as other PC brand companies did. In the process, Dell computers lost their uniqueness in the eyes of consumers in this competitive market. Second, think about the notebook-sized Macintosh computer called the PowerBook 100 that Apple introduced in 1991. Apple enlisted Japanese consumer electronics giant Sony to design and manufacture this notebook computer for both the U.S. and Japanese markets. Sony was long known for its expertise in miniaturization and was a supplier of disk drives, monitors and power supplies to Apple for various Macintosh models. In the PC industry, where technology changes quickly and existing products become obsolete in a short period of time, the window of business opportunity is naturally limited. Therefore, Apple's inclination was to outsource the production of its notebook computer in order to introduce it in markets around the world as soon as possible, before competition picked up. However, this outsourcing relationship did not last long, as Apple became concerned about a technology loss to Sony. Third, consider Sony's own more recent struggle with its worldwide recall of lithium-ion batteries for notebook computers used by Dell, Apple and Lenovo, and its postponement of the European release of the PlayStation 3 game system due to delays in the production of blue laser diodes, a key component of Blu-ray disc players. Sony was once a paragon of technological excellence and product creativity in the highly competitive Japanese electronics industry. One explanation for Sony's recent crises is attributed to the trend of outsourcing to electronics manufacturing services companies to cut costs. As a result, Sony has lost consumer confidence and market share.

These examples highlight some negative consequences of outsourcing strategy. Our research seems to show that there is an optimal level of outsourcing for all companies, whether in manufacturing or in services – although exactly what that optimum is differs significantly both from one firm to the next and over time. Indeed, we found that initial outsourcing helps improve profitability; but because of this initial success, companies tend to overdo it, resulting in lower performance, thus forcing them to reconsider the virtue of their outsourcing strategies. Of course, neither executives nor academics can get it right all the time, but we still believe there are important lessons to be learned.

A balanced perspective

What is the right outsourcing strategy for a given firm? In observing that many firms do not outsource all their activities but instead use both insourcing and outsourcing, one could argue that these firms are attempting to strike the most effective balance between insourcing and outsourcing to leverage the benefits and mitigate the costs. We know outsourcing can provide advantages, especially when a firm cannot perform certain activities as well as potential suppliers. But outsourcing has drawbacks, too. First, firms often compete for and avail of the most promising outsourcing options, leaving less productive outsourcing options when they engage more intensively in outsourcing. Second, as increased outsourcing demands more managerial attention and frequently constrains managerial resources, it may lead to inadequate oversight of outsourcing activities. Third, increased outsourcing increases transaction and bureaucratic costs to a point where these start to exceed production cost gains. And fourth, firms that outsource component technologies may start to forget their own existing knowledge, as well as incur the opportunity costs of no longer being able to learn about changes in these technologies. These all result in a slower and inadequate response to the evolving needs (or demands) of consumers.

Furthermore, although firms can potentially gain access to a new technology through outsourcing, this does not guarantee that they will be able to integrate the technology into their existing business processes and deploy it in the marketplace. The first reason is that firms' internal capabilities cannot be substituted by outsourcing, since passive capability accumulation is unlikely to occur. Second, comprehending customers' user experience with a new technology depends on various interdependent, tacit processes, which may be interrupted when activities are decoupled across internal and external suppliers. Also, learning about customer preferences requires successive modifications, which demands frequent updating and renegotiation of outsourcing contracts.

As the examples of Dell, Apple and Sony presented earlier amply illustrate, upstream outsourcing strategy affects downstream marketing performance, including product quality, product delivery, consumer confidence, brand equity and even corporate reputation. The academic literature equally suggests that a misalignment (i.e., a wrong governance choice in the circumstances facing the firm) leads to a decrease in performance. In other words, making the wrong decision by outsourcing activities that are best kept in-house or integrating activities that are best outsourced is a costly mistake. Our research attests to that and proves that any firm is best off by choosing a mix of outsourcing and insourcing. More specifically, we show that outsourcing has a negative curvilinear, U-shaped relationship with marketing performance. This implies that as firms outsource more and more of their activities, they improve their performance – first by quite a lot but gradually by less and less; until they reach the optimal point, beyond which more outsourcing leads to lower performance – first a little lower, but eventually a lot lower.

A balanced perspective on using both outsourcing and insourcing offers insights on the sourcing strategy-performance relationship. The underlying argument of a balanced perspective is that firms that outsource all of their activities run into a multitude of problems, such as a gradual loss of their own innovative capabilities and bargaining power *vis-à-vis* suppliers and their products' loss of distinctiveness in the eyes of the customer. However, firms that only insource fail to use the powerful incentives supplied by market forces, thus becoming bureaucratic and inefficient. Therefore, outsourcing some but not all activities provides the best solution overall and there is thus an optimal degree of outsourcing. In other words, firms should strike the most effective balance between outsourcing and insourcing to capitalize on their benefits and mitigate their costs.[21]

In other words, failing to strike a balance between outsourcing and insourcing and instead outsourcing too much may contribute to lower performance, for the following reasons. First, firms often compete for and enter into the most promising outsourcing options, thus leaving less productive outsourcing options when they outsource more. Second, increased outsourcing requires more managerial attention and constrains internal managerial resources, thus leading to inadequate oversight of outsourcing activities. Third, more outsourcing increases transaction and bureaucratic costs beyond a point where they outweigh the benefits.[22]

---

[21]   Frank T. Rothaermel, Michael A. Hitt and Lloyd A. Jobe, "Balancing Vertical Integration and Strategic Outsourcing: Effects on Product Portfolio, Product Success, and Firm Performance," *Strategic Management Journal*, 27, 2006: 1033–56.

[22]   Masaaki Kotabe, Michael J. Mol, Janet Y. Murray and Ronaldo Parente, "Outsourcing and its Implications for Market Success: Negative

We believe a similar line of reasoning can apply to the internationali-zation of sourcing (i.e., onshoring and offshoring) and how that affects performance. More specifically, there are advantages and disadvantages associated with global sourcing, as we highlighted above. As a firm does more offshoring (particularly offshore outsourcing), the disadvantages become greater to the point where they severely impede performance. If firms do not use offshoring at all, they cannot enjoy any of the advantages of offshoring, such as a wider supply base from which to choose and lower costs.

Oliver Williamson, a Nobel laureate in transaction cost economics, distin-guishes between production and transaction costs.[23] "Production costs" are the costs of producing a good or service; and "transaction costs" are all the costs incurred as the product moves from one supply chain partner to the next. When firms use offshore outsourcing by procuring from foreign suppliers, it may help reduce their production costs. In some instances, a local supplier's production costs may be lower than those of foreign suppliers, but this is often the exception and not the rule. Transaction costs, on the other hand, tend to be higher for such offshoring, as there are many institutional, cultural and language barriers that must be overcome.

The cost of searching for supply sources abroad – whether internal or external sources – is somewhat higher than that for local supply sources. The cost of evaluating those foreign supply sources is also much higher, as the evaluation costs are strongly related to the familiarity that decision-makers have with the other party. Since firms are likely to be less familiar with foreign supply sources and decision-makers may be unable to draw on their networks in helping them evaluate these sources, this incurs substantial evaluation costs.

We argue that offshoring is a balancing act between production and transaction costs. Firms need to find the proper balance between domes-tic and foreign supply sources (using onshoring and offshoring) if they wish to locate at the top of the curve and obtain the highest possible performance. They can achieve this by using foreign sources for some,

Curvilinearity, Firm Resources, and Competition," *Journal of the Academy of Marketing Science*, 40, March 2012: 329–46.

23   Oliver E. Williamson, *The Economic Institutions of Capitalism* (New York: Free Press, 1995).

but not all, of their sourcing. Sourcing everything from abroad produces poor performance results because the disadvantages of offshoring, as in the hollowing-out argument, become too large. Focusing all efforts on onshoring, however, is a serious form of myopia with equally disastrous effects for firm performance, primarily because the firm is not capitalizing on important opportunities to improve competitiveness. An illustration of our argument on achieving a balance between outsourcing and insourcing (offshoring and onshoring) is presented in Figure 4.1.

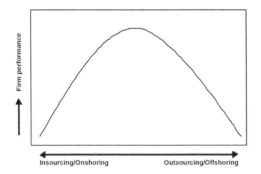

Figure 4.1   An inverted u-shaped relationship between the degree of global outsourcing and firm performance

The balanced perspective is therefore summarized as follows: some activities are best outsourced globally, while others should be insourced globally (from a performance perspective). A firm can enjoy optimal performance when it correctly outsources and insources all activities. Similarly, the firm should also balance onshoring and offshoring activities. This produces the pattern of an inverted U-shaped (negatively curvilinear) relationship between outsourcing (offshoring) and performance, with the top of the curve presenting the performance optimum.

The role of firm resources and the level of competition

Our studies show that the optimal level of marketing performance varies with the strength of a firm's internal resources. As you would expect, firms with a stronger resource base tend to rely more on their internal resources and thus outsource less for optimal performance. Firms with weaknesses in their resource base *vis-à-vis* competitors are better off by outsourcing, whereas those with stronger resources can afford to keep more activities in-house. In measuring those resources, we examined whether firms have highly productive resources and whether they manage to create the kinds of products that sell well in competitive overseas markets.

Competition effectively represents the seriousness of the challenges facing a firm when it seeks to market its products. In general, where competition is more intense, firms tend to and should outsource more. This is the case because competition forces firms to constantly search for cost efficiencies, which may be obtained through outsourcing. But equally, some research also suggests that outsourcing increases levels of competition. As shown in the Dell case, this effect arises as outsourcing tends to remove the distinctiveness of a firm's product offerings. Thus, its product differentiation capability is reduced because all competing firms rely on a similar set of suppliers for their inputs.

We found optimal outsourcing levels to be lower with high R&D investment and marketing-related expenditures, as these tend to reduce competition in the industry by building innovative capability and brand reputation. Similarly, the more concentrated (i.e., oligopolistic) the industry is, the less competitive it is and the less firms in the industry should outsource. So, any reduced competitive pressure alleviates firms' need to outsource activities in order to seek cost efficiencies.

As noted above, these are not the only factors that determine how much firms should outsource. The best outsourcing strategy also depends on the context. Over time, with standardization of components and lower transportation and communication costs, firms can outsource more. Location also matters a great deal. U.S. companies tend to believe that knowledge is divisible. Out of curiosity, I went to Japan and conducted an informal study with executives there, and found that they tend to believe that knowledge is less divisible. In similar executive programs, I found that European executives also tend to think that knowledge is less divisible. From an American point of view, Europeans and Japanese appear risk averse, as they do not outsource as much.

Costly wrong outsourcing decision

Using a firm's market share as a proxy for its performance, we conducted a further formal study[24] to explore how outsourcing levels affect a firm's market share. This helps us better understand how strongly a firm's outsourcing decisions affect its market share. We did this by statistically predicting the firm's market share with all the variables at their means and then varying outsourcing from very low to very high levels (i.e., all the way from the bottom 2.3 percent to the top 2.3 percent levels).

The results demonstrate that the impact of making the "wrong" outsourcing decision is significant, as firms' predicted market shares sink substantially at both the bottom and the top end of outsourcing levels and drop by over 20 percent in some extreme cases. For a large majority of firms, the results are rather less dramatic, of course. In all, among our sample of firms, the optimal outsourcing strategy for the "average" firm was actually to outsource slightly more than it did.

Executives' perspectives

Our qualitative fieldwork[25] in the automobile industry presents a similar picture to this statistical research and is in line with our main idea that as firms deviate further from their optimal degree of outsourcing by either insourcing or outsourcing too much, their performance will suffer disproportionately. As stated by one top executive from Ford:

> We need to constantly monitor our relationship with our module suppliers. It is complicated to figure out what is too much or too little when it comes to restructuring a traditional manufacturing plant to implement a modular production approach that involves a high degree of outsourcing activities.

---

[24]   Michael J. Mol and Masaaki Kotabe, "Overcoming Inertia: Drivers of the Outsourcing Process," *Long Range Planning*, 44 (May), 2011: 160–78.

[25]   Masaaki Kotabe, Ronaldo Parente and Janet Y. Murray, "Antecedents and Outcomes of Modular Production in the Brazilian Automobile Industry: A Grounded Theory Approach," *Journal of International Business Studies*, 38(1), 2007: 84–106.

Pushing to higher levels of outsourcing may also have negative outcomes:

> These higher levels of outsourcing are taking up most of our managers' time …
> It requires extremely high levels of supervision to keep our suppliers perform-
> ing at higher levels for all the activities we have suppliers performing for us …
> There are many unanticipated costs we are dealing with …

Yet another plant manager at Volkswagen, while emphasizing the importance of outsourcing as a way to save costs, suggested that it is very important to know the optimal level of outsourcing: "We developed a modular
consortium [using outsourcing] … that requires us to know what activities to outsource and what not to outsource." In general, our respondents
recognized the benefits of outsourcing, but were also concerned about
its potential downside and their ability to decide on the optimal level of
outsourcing.

We found in our interviews that there seems to be evidence of diminishing returns from outsourcing in the automobile industry. In general, the
executives whom we interviewed suggested that their firm's competitive
advantage was linked to decisions regarding how well the firm structured
its methods of production and supply chain. As one respondent said: "It
is hard to completely evaluate all costs involved with outsourcing and the
potential for product quality problems, delivery schedule problems, and
large price adjustments on the supply side." Therefore, there seems to
be an optimal level of outsourcing activities beyond which diminishing
returns set in. As stated by another respondent:

> We have a daily meeting with all our suppliers, so that we [can] predict and
> identify any potential problems … and make quick [fine tuning] adjustments
> to the extent we depend on our suppliers…. The key is to find the optimal level
> of dependency [in outsourcing] that we can afford.

Our fieldwork indicates that auto suppliers are providing more and more
complete systems through outsourcing, and are also increasing their
engagement in engineering design and development. According to one
plant manager at General Motors: "Our strategy focuses on leveraging our
capabilities with the suppliers' capabilities through outsourcing … in our
case many suppliers … have been involved in the project since the design
phase [and] are working together from the project conception." But while
outsourcing seems to be necessary and has some positive implications,

the risk of overexposure through a lack of balance between insourcing and outsourcing is also clear, according to another executive:

> It is important that we leverage our capabilities [with those of suppliers] through the codesign of components and systems, … but we must find the balance between how much to transfer to the supplier side and how much to keep in-house … any miscalculations can lead to problems and compromise our competitiveness.

Lessons learned

We believe that there is a relationship between outsourcing and firm performance in the form of a firm's market share. Therefore, from a decision-maker's perspective, it is important to understand how outsourcing affects market share and to know that firms can only benefit from outsourcing up to a point.

The first lesson is that firms that do not properly balance their outsourcing and insourcing levels will suffer in terms of market share, regardless of whatever other efforts they may undertake in marketing their products. The rationale for this is that if a firm clearly outsources too little, it will not achieve the cost levels its customers are seeking; while outsourcing too much leads to a loss of distinctiveness in the eyes of the customer.

Second, decision-makers in charge of supply chain in a firm with strong resources can afford to outsource relatively little; this is also true if the firm operates in a less competitive environment.

Third, we would strongly urge executives to have some direct involvement in outsourcing decisions. Firms that decide on their outsourcing levels without properly considering the consequences of those decisions for their market-oriented activities are likely to come to misguided conclusions; therefore, some level of integration of information between the different functions of the firm is essential.

The key practical implication of our research is for executives to be wary about the effects of either too much or too little outsourcing, as this will have a detrimental impact on their firm's market share, and ultimately its chances of survival in the marketplace. Our theory suggests that the optimal amount of outsourcing is highly context dependent, both temporally and spatially; and in addition, it varies from one firm to another. Perhaps, firms in our sample have now, on average, gone beyond their optimal degree of outsourcing and are suffering performance losses as a consequence. And, of course, few if any firms are "average," so an individual firm should always consider its own idiosyncrasies.

Conclusions and managerial implications

Based on our discussions, executives should reconsider and redesign their global outsourcing activities. Many executives have a strong general idea of what constitutes a sound outsourcing and offshoring policy. They recognize that outsourcing and offshoring every activity may lead to disasters; they also realize that not all activities should be insourced and onshored (i.e., brought back to the home country).

There is a current tendency in practice to describe outsourcing or offshoring performance problems as "implementation issues." Executives often think that their outsourcing or offshoring decision is the appropriate design choice, and tend to attribute undesirable performance to various implementation problems that occur when dealing with independent and overseas suppliers. We would suggest that there are many more fundamental problems of outsourcing or offshoring that are unrelated to implementation problems. Rather, there are limits to outsourcing and offshoring, and many inputs of a firm should not be outsourced or offshored.

Executives are often not conscious of the fact that there is an optimal degree of outsourcing and offshoring across their entire portfolio. Instead, they tend to see the good or evil of outsourcing or offshoring particular items or activities, in that suppliers are not well equipped, insufficient guarantees are built into contracts or market circumstances change rapidly. Many firms do not conduct sufficient analysis before jumping into outsourcing or offshoring. This helps explain why, in practice, outsourcing or offshoring often looks like a bandwagoning process. If one firm increases outsourcing, other firms will follow suit without careful analysis, unaware of whether this will be a good move.

Outsourcing and insourcing provide complementary knowledge across different stages of a firm's value chain. Consequently, firms do not outsource their entire production, especially in times of technological change. If firms engage in too much outsourcing of technologies, they may risk not having the opportunity to learn about changes in these technologies through insourcing. Therefore, the benefits of outsourcing or offshoring will materialize only when a firm has the organizational capacity to integrate outsourced and/or offshored items/activities into its operations. In addition, many firms make outsourcing or offshoring decisions by evaluating a handful of options based on their previous experience and by following their competitors.

Executives are in need of guidelines as to where the optimal point lies for their particular business at a particular time. Based on the contingency approach, the following indicators help answer that question: asset specificity, uncertainty, firm competencies, industry trends and firm nationality and location. These moderating factors may help determine what is optimal for a particular firm at a specific point in time. Indeed, a firm's capabilities can change its production costs and its governance costs relative to the market.[26] As a result, the frontier at which outsourcing gives way to insourcing shifts over time. Timing is crucial, as the optimal point will shift due to changes both internal and external to the firm.

From a managerial perspective, developing a model that helps determine a firm's optimal degree of outsourcing or offshoring would be very useful. Based on this model, executives could prioritize their activities and outsource or offshore until they more or less reach optimality. As global sourcing is a dynamic process, competing firms may not accurately grasp the full benefits (and costs) of outsourcing or offshoring activities due to causal ambiguity. Furthermore, firms face a unique set of internal and external factors that affect their optimal level of outsourcing and offshoring. Therefore, simply following the first-mover's current outsourcing or offshoring strategy offers no guarantee for improved performance. Instead, tackling that challenge involves a broader behavioral understanding of how firms' outsourcing or offshoring trajectories change over time and within industries.

---

[26]   Amit Jain and Raymond-Alain Thietart, "Capabilities as Shift Parameters for the Outsourcing Decision," *Strategic Management Journal,* 35, 2014: 1881–90.

Summary

Global sourcing strategy has gained momentum since the core competency argument was popularized in the 1990s. Managerial attention gradually shifted from insourcing to outsourcing. If this is taken to the theoretical extreme, a firm should focus on its core competency and outsource everything else. However, what constitutes core competency is not always clear. If this is defined narrowly, the firm will become vulnerable to changes in technology and market needs. If this is defined broadly, the firm will end up investing more in in-house development and production than is necessary.

As a result, one can make arguments for and against outsourcing. Arguments for outsourcing generally look to the short-term benefits of lower fixed investment, resulting in a lower breakeven point and higher profitability; while arguments against outsourcing focus on the long-term implications of gradually losing technological knowledge and capabilities. Therefore, finding the optimum insourcing/outsourcing level requires a balancing act. However, it is not easy to determine the optimal level in practice, due primarily to differences in firm resources and levels of competition.

5 Lessons from the consumer electronics industry[1]

Introduction

History will always teach us valuable lessons. In this chapter, instead of looking at global supply chain management through a snapshot in time, we examine its evolution from a historical point of view. The consumer electronics (CE) industry offers great insight into the dynamics of supply chain management over time on a global basis. No discussion of CE firms would be complete without a brief introduction to the dynamics underpinning the industry in the years when the specter of global competition first appeared. The worldwide CE industry has seen strong international competition since the 1950s. The Western world dominated the field until this time, when competition began to emerge from Japan, starting with the export of transistors. Very soon, Japanese CE firms such as Sony and Panasonic became a force to reckon with. In particular, rivalry in television technology became especially fierce in the 1970s. It is difficult to pinpoint exactly when global competition became so intense among firms in the Triad region. But in 1951, when Japan's Ministry of International Trade and Industry (MITI) permitted Japanese companies to enter into licensing agreements for television technology with foreign firms, several Japanese companies signed pacts with U.S. companies, such as the Radio Corporation of America (RCA). At the time, MITI expected to receive only a few applications for approval, but it ended up authorizing around

---

[1]   This chapter is adapted from Masaaki Kotabe, Michael J. Mol and Sonia Ketkar, "An Evolutionary Stage Model of Outsourcing and Competence Destruction: A Triad Comparison of the Consumer Electronics Industry," *Management International Review*, 48(1), 2008: 65–93.

37 applications.[2] As electrical goods rapidly permeated Japanese society, local companies expanded and developed a competitive edge based on a quick learning process and low labor costs.

U.S. companies such as Emerson Radio, RCA, Zenith and Magnavox also realized that they could gain a cost-based competitive advantage by subcontracting first assembly and later manufacturing operations to their Asian partners at lower cost. Hence, in the 1960s and 1970s, outsourcing became popular with many U.S. firms. In subsequent years, Japanese CE firms acquired technology from U.S. companies, gained technological competency and launched new technologically advanced products derived from their own research and development (R&D). Competition between U.S. firms and their Japanese counterparts heated up when Japanese firms entered the U.S. domestic market and began selling their products at lower prices. This led U.S. firms to accuse the Japanese firms of dumping. The developments in the industry that followed show that U.S. companies rapidly increased outsourcing and in turn their dependence on their Japanese partners – first for radios and subsequently for television sets. By the end of the 1960s, there were no U.S. radio manufacturers left in the United States.

A discussion of the European CE industry is mostly an account of Philips and its activities. Probably only one other company, Thomson of France, was as active in the industry – more so than firms such as Siemens and Telefunken. Like some U.S. firms (National Union Electric, Zenith), European firms felt threatened by Japanese competition in the CE industry. Prompted by a turbulent environment post the 1970s and lobbying from influential firms like Philips for protection from non-European rivals, Europe implemented new policies. European CE firms were also granted subsidies. Especially in the 1980s, the European Union (EU) stepped in to defend against Japanese penetration of EU markets. Nevertheless, the European CE industry went through a series of restructurings in the 1990s, like the major turnaround "Operation Centurion" at Philips.

To illustrate the intensity of this rivalry and firms' attempts to outdo each other through innovation and imitation, let us consider this example. As

---

[2]   Simon Partner, *Assembled in Japan: Electrical Goods and the Making of the Japanese Consumer* (Berkeley, CA: University of California Press, 1999).

the story goes, in 1963, Philips gave the world the audiocassette, which was a noise reduction innovation because Philips managed to eliminate the background tape sound. Based on this product, in 1964, a Sony employee proposed the idea of a videocassette. In 1976, Sony introduced its Betamax videocassette recorder (VCR) in the United States. In late 1977, RCA launched its own VHS SelectaVision VCR format, which was made by Matsushita (renamed as Panasonic in 2008). This product was an improvement on Sony's Betamax, which could record for only an hour. Thus, an innovation/product introduction by one firm was very quickly followed by the creation of another entrant which sought to gain market share. In this chapter, we historically examine the corporate strategies, trials and tribulations of three companies – Emerson Radio (United States), Royal Philips Electronics (Netherlands) and Sony Corp. (Japan) – in the field of CE. We focus on firm decisions related to entertainment product groups – namely audio, video and television products. Every product introduction built on and upgraded previous technology. The three companies in our sample have changed their corporate strategies innumerable times in the last 30 to 40 years, sometimes dramatically so. We focus on those strategies that are relevant to outsourcing.

All three firms were technological pioneers at some point in the early days of CE. While Emerson Radio discovered a way to retain its market share by supplying CE products at low prices, Philips became Europe's core consumer electronics learning base and Sony revolutionized the industry with its miniaturization of CE products. So, how did these firms acquire technological competences? And why did they start losing their technical prowess?

Overview of three companies

Emerson Radio

Emerson Radio evolved from a pioneer and maker of CE products to a distributor. The company's history is complex because it changed ownership a few times. Emerson Radio & Phonograph, as the company was originally called by founder Max Abrams in 1922, mass-produced radios around the time of the Second World War. Its radios were very modern for the time and were decorative in appearance. It also manufactured phonographs and televisions. In 1965, it was taken over by National Union

Corp. (NUC); and in 1975, Major Corp (a phonograph manufacturer founded in 1956) bought the brand name for CE from NUC and changed its own name to Emerson Radio.

Emerson Radio obtained technology mainly through its own efforts and through acquisitions. Soon after entering the radio business, the company introduced the first radio-phonograph combination sold in the United States. In 1932, it launched its popular miniature radio, which was around 8.5 by 6.25 inches; and it soon became the leader in the manufacture and sale of miniature radios. By 1938, it had sold over 1 million of these radios. In 1954 – years before Japan's Sony became famous for the miniaturization of CE products – Emerson Radio introduced the tiniest radio to date, measuring 3.5 by 3.75 inches. This achievement made Emerson Radio the leading producer of tiny radios in the world. It was so technologically advanced in the 1950s that it planned to "build a radio, using transistors instead of tubes, so small that it can be worn like a wrist watch."[3] After the Second World War, it also introduced one of the first television sets in the U.S., causing earnings to more than double by the mid-1950s. Emerson Radio also had R&D labs in the United States. By this time, Emerson Radio had a solid brand name and superior technological capabilities; and it attempted to capture nearby markets, mainly in Canada and Latin America. However, as more players entered the emerging television industry, competition at home increased and Emerson started cutting the prices of its television sets in order to survive in the market. It was around this time that the company realized it needed to take drastic measures to subsist in the industry, and it duly did so (discussed below). In 1953, Emerson Radio launched the first compatible color television receiver; and in 1958, it acquired further technological capabilities when it bought CE inventor DuMont's television, phonograph and high-fidelity stereo equipment operations. By the early 1960s, Emerson Radio had developed sophisticated production capabilities complemented by a strong brand name in CE. But even then, in the battle for market share and under the onslaught from foreign CE firms, U.S. producers like Emerson Radio were fast losing market share. In the latter half of the 1960s, as American companies such as RCA, Westinghouse Electric, Admiral and General Electric struggled to hang on to their businesses, Emerson continued

---

[3]   "In Tune with Emerson," *Forbes*, June 15, 1954, pp. 22–23.

making a profit.[4] Emerson built a large customer base and acquired a significant portion of the market by eventually setting up cost-efficient manufacturing operations in East Asia to deliver electronic products at reasonable prices to middle-class American citizens. It was one of the very first U.S. companies to popularize such manufacturing strategies. In the short run, profitability grew; but in the long run, it faced several problems due to excessive outsourcing.

Philips Electronics

Philips was established in the Netherlands in 1912 and grew to become the largest European CE company and one of the largest in the world. Its main activity was electrical lighting, but it acquired a leading position in CE before the mid-1970s, when Japanese companies began to enter Europe. From its inception, Philips was based on R&D and developed its own technologies, mostly keeping R&D in-house in various labs across Europe. This enabled it to increase its own product portfolio from the 1920s. However, during the Second World War, several of its European operations were destroyed. Postwar Philips enhanced its technical capabilities by relying on color television technology licensed from RCA like most of the Japanese CE firms in the 1970s. At the same time, Philips' research efforts proved to be beneficial for Japan's Matsushita because Philips owned 35 percent of Matsushita, which depended on Philips' R&D. Philips entered into collaborations and joint ventures for innovation and new product development in the 1980s. Its most successful collaboration was with Sony to launch the compact disc (CD) system. However, by the late 1990s, Philips had lost its once superior technological capabilities.

Sony Corporation

Although Sony did not invent the transistor, it was the first company to launch the transistor radio – an innovative feat which played a major role in Sony's emergence as a technological leader. Founded in 1953, Tokyo Tsushin – as the company was originally called before its name was changed to Sony – quickly built a reputation for itself in Japan and soon in the rest of the world. In 1953, Sony signed a pact with U.S.-based Western

---

4   "Emerson Perseveres with Heart Device," *New York Times*, October 19, 1981: 4.

Electric to share its transistor technology and then conducted its own research on radios. In 1955, Sony introduced its first transistor radio, the TR-55, to the market. Like Sony, other U.S. and Japanese manufacturers had developed their own versions of the transistor radio around the same time and sold those in the U.S. market. However, in the international arena, Sony had to compete not only with other Japanese contenders but also with U.S. and European players, which already had brand equity and established distribution networks. In 1982, Sony introduced the TV Walkman, a technological breakthrough in those days. Throughout this era, Sony, like most other Japanese companies, relied on in-house R&D, continually increasing R&D spend over the years – for instance, this rose by 9.6 percent in 1983 to $90.6 million. Again, like most other Japanese CE firms, Sony initially followed a conservative policy by keeping R&D in-house; but it eventually gave in to financial concerns (brought about by an inability to meet high demand and fierce rivalry) and resorted to outsourcing. Hence, the 1990s saw it "shift from a technology-based company to a product-based company," in the words of Ken Kutaragi, president of Sony Computer Entertainment Corp.

In the next section, we examine the dynamic shifts, in four different stages, in the sourcing strategies employed by Emerson, Philips and Sony. Table 5.1 contains a summary.

Table 5.1   Evolution of outsourcing strategy

	Firm Characteristics	Trigger	Stage 1	Stage 2	Stage 3	Stage 4
Emerson (1922)	R&D Centralized Manufacturing – Decentralized	Increased cost competition	Outsourcing deals with U.S.'s Admiral and East Asian manufacturers	Fall out with Admiral and complete reliance on foreign original equipment manufacturers (OEMs). Emerson in charge of design but not manufacture	Realization of the loss of technology to East Asian OEMs	Complete reliance on outsourcing, unrelated diversification
Phillips (1912)	R&D Centralized Manufacturing – Decentralized	Increased cost competition	Setting up manufacturing subsidiaries in Taiwan, etc. (1980s)	Selling its foreign factories and increased outsourcing from Taiwan and Korea (1980s)	Loss of DVD technology to Japanese (1990s)	Increased R&D in-house, and stepped up outsourcing as well (1990s)
Sony (1953)	R&D Centralized Manufacturing – Centralized	Increased cost competition	Setting up manufacturing subsidiaries in the US, Brazil, Taiwain, etc. (1970s)	Selling some of its manufacturing plans to Solectron; and more outsourcing to independent manufacturers (1990s)	Realization of the loss of innovative capabilities (2003)	Reduced outsourcing for high-tech components and increased in-house production of high-demand products (2000s)

Evolution of offshoring strategy

Stage 1: offshore sourcing (setting up foreign subsidiaries in low-cost locations)

Before plunging headlong into the establishment of foreign manufacturing subsidiaries, CE firms dabbled in foreign transactions. After Emerson faced difficulties selling its television sets amid tough competition, and after trying out a price-cutting strategy, the company found another way to increase profits: by lowering costs. In 1956, sales fell from over $87 million to $74 million, while earnings were a meager $84 850. The company then started to set up cost-efficient manufacturing operations in East Asia in the 1960s.

Philips, on the other hand, had been collaborating with foreign companies since 1916, when it partnered with General Electric to exchange technical know-how and experience. Although the company had been engaged in foreign trade activities, foreign investment was not established until in the 1920s. Philips moved many of its production plants out of the Netherlands to avoid high tariffs, causing unemployment at home. This was the first time the company set up offshore production. In the following years, Philips closed down more plants in the Netherlands. It followed an aggressive expansionist policy over the next decade and established several subsidiaries in different parts of the world. By the late 1960s, Philips had manufacturing operations in several corners of the globe, including Singapore, Indonesia, South Africa and Kenya. Almost all of these places were low-cost locations. In 1968, the company's profits rose by 10 percent. In 1970, Philips set up operations in low-cost Taiwan, where it began the production of monochrome picture tubes; by 1989, this facility had become the world's largest tube manufacturer and Philips had a total of five plants in Taiwan. In 1974, the company discontinued its non-color picture tube production in the United Kingdom and moved production to low-cost locations. Around this time, CE companies the world over were involved in similar moves to low-cost regions for manufacturing. By 1974, Philips already had television and audio plants in Singapore, a black-and-white television plant in Taiwan, a stereo plant in Brazil and an electronics production plant in South Korea.

Philips suffered a setback in profits in the fourth quarter of 1975. This also marked a turning point for Philips, as it faced tough competition from

Japanese competitors. Philips' video technology, V2000, was in direct competition with the Japanese VCR systems, Beta and VHS. By the end of the 1970s, the Japanese companies had entered Europe and formed partnerships and collaborations, which helped them gain a foothold and market share in Europe. Although the V2000 format developed by Philips was technologically superior to the Japanese VCR systems, it failed – partly due to Philips' inability to find partners.[5] This marked the beginning of a collaborative era for Philips, during which it went on an alliance spree and partnered with several foreign firms. Philips increased its presence in Japan by buying a stake in Marantz in 1980 from U.S.-based Superscope, which had owned a majority stake in the company. Marantz, then owned by Philips, soon became its base in Japan for the production of goods at low cost. As time went by, Philips – like other CE firms – spread itself over several low-cost regions, enabling it to compete more efficiently in the industry.

Sony set up its first foreign production plant, the Champagne Plant, in 1959 in Hong Kong. This was a transistor radio assembly plant established through a local firm that provided all the capital and managed the business. Sony had a contractual agreement with it for production. Goods made at the plant (mainly assembled transistor radios) were then sent to Europe, Australia, Canada and other areas. However, Sony shut down the plant in 1961 due to an undisclosed "disagreement" with the local firm, making this an unsuccessful first move abroad. Compared to most U.S. firms, Sony was much later in moving its operations. Competition in the industry compelled it to set up several foreign plants in the 1970s. In 1973, Sony established Sony do Brazil. That same year, Sony also denied reports that it would second source products from National Semicon. By 1973, Sony was manufacturing radios, black-and-white televisions and tape recorders through its Sony Korea subsidiary. It also formed a joint venture with a Korean partner, Hwasin Industries, for the production of color televisions. Following a drop in overall sales, Sony reorganized its distribution network. Other foreign subsidiaries set up in the 1970s and 1980s included audio manufacturing subsidiary Sony da Amazonia in Brazil; a VCR factory in Taiwan; a VHS plant in Malaysia; audio tape manufacturing subsidiary Magneticos de Mexico; a joint venture with

---

5   Xiudian Dai, *Corporate Strategy, Public Policy and New Technologies: Philips and the Consumer Electronics Industry* (Bingley: Emerald Group Publishing, 1996).

Motoradio, Sony Videobras, for video tape manufacturing; and several others worldwide. It also established Sony Precision Engineering Center in Singapore to manufacture optical pickups for CD players and joint production of CE products with a Chinese trading firm. Most of these offshore plants were in low-cost locations and involved joint production with local partners.

Until the late 1980s, Sony kept R&D in Japan. By 1988, it had considerably increased offshore production. The company claimed that the appreciation of the yen prompted it to expand overseas production because this made it less profitable to manufacture goods in Japan. In the 1980s, around 20 percent of Sony's production was undertaken by foreign plants and the company felt the need to further expand manufacturing overseas. Sony aimed to develop its Asian plants as supply centers for high-technology products. The company hoped that it would undertake at least 35 percent of manufacturing outside of Japan in the 1990s. Thus, it sought to increase offshore production in the 1980s. However, in 1985, Sony announced that it would start shifting its focus from CE to business customers in response to a fall in profits. In 1989, it also started setting up regional R&D and engineering centers, such as the Advanced Video Technology Center, a development base for high-definition television in San Jose in the United States. By the first half of the 1990s, Sony had over 20 R&D centers outside Japan.

During this stage, all three firms perceived the need to lower manufacturing costs. Philips and Sony responded to this need by setting up plants in low-cost locations – as did their industry rivals. Emerson seemed to opt for sourcing components and then final products directly from overseas manufacturers which were low-cost producers. CE firms often followed each other to low-cost destinations in Asia, overturning each other's temporary gains and then re-entering the race to reduce costs even further. Nevertheless, this opening move to low-cost regions seemed to be successful, as profits initially rose in all three cases. However, the relentless pursuit of advanced technologies soon prompted CE firms to reduce costs even further, which characterizes Stage 2 of our model.

Stage 2: phasing out (transferring production to independent operators)

U.S.-based Emerson Radio moved through the stages of our model much faster than the other two firms. After the takeover by NUC, Emerson Radio continued to produce television sets and other CE products. However, sales were low and profits remained elusive. Emerson Radio began operating in the red under NUC, apparently because it had too little volume to cover fixed costs. Between 1967 and 1971, the division lost about $27 million. In order to reduce fixed costs, NUC outsourced the manufacturing of Emerson Radio's CE products to U.S.-based Admiral Corp. Under this pact, Emerson Radio was responsible for designing, engineering and marketing. At the same time, Emerson also imported home entertainment products and some other CE goods from East Asian manufacturers. However, in 1973, Admiral terminated its contract with Emerson Radio, which was thereafter dependent almost entirely on Asian original equipment manufacturers for its products.

Philips experienced its own share of problems and after profits took a beating in 1975, it was encouraged to further lower its fixed costs by increasing its reliance on offshore manufacturers. The company continued to phase out production in higher-cost locations, such as its color television manufacturing plant in Canada, and moved further production offshore. In 1981, it set up its seventh factory in Singapore for the production of radios and increased its investment in product development and automation in Singapore; it also set up an audio equipment plant in China in 1985.

In 1980, Philips restructured its organization. The V2000 debacle had hit Philips hard. Before then, it was a prosperous organization; but following the failure of its V2000, profitability fell. At the time, it introduced its make-or-buy policy. Under this new policy, the company withdrew from certain industries, such as military and defense. The company, which thus far had been locally responsive in its various markets, started moving to globalize its businesses, divesting non-core operations and entering into joint ventures for production. In the late 1980s, Philips' chief executive officer (CEO) clarified the company's new direction, stating: "On a world scale, you must be selective and stick to what you can do best." Philips also sold its white goods unit to Whirlpool and its minicomputers unit to Digital Equipment. Under its agreement with Whirlpool, Whirlpool was to own 53 percent of the joint venture with Philips, but it soon bought out

Philips' entire stake in the company. Philips continued to sell white goods until the 1990s, when it disengaged from the business entirely. In 1981, Philips spun off electronics parts subsidiary Cambridge; and in a series of sales a few years later, it sold two more electronics component units to Cambridge Electronics Industries. In 1981, Sanyo acquired Philips' U.K. color television production plant to sell its own color television sets. In 1983, after the failure of its V2000, Philips bought VHS models from Japan and sold them in Australia and New Zealand. North American Philips (NAP), Philips' U.S. subsidiary, purchased television sets from Matsushita for sale in the United States under the Magnavox, Philco and Sylvania brands. Japan's Pioneer was also supplying CD players to NAP. Matsushita also supplied VCRs to be sold in the United States under the Magnavox brand. Thus, NAP was entirely dependent on products supplied by Japanese companies.

What is notable about Philips' strategies is its proclivity to enter into joint ventures. After the 1980s, the company ended up with many pacts with foreign CE companies for joint production or R&D in Asia. Significant examples include joint production of VHS recorders in South Korea with Dong Won Electronics and a CD player venture with Shenzhen Shen Fei Laser of China. These allowed the partner in the venture to learn from the more technologically advanced Philips. Philips gradually increased its reliance on these partners and in many cases the partners ultimately took over operations from Philips. Philips had a videodisc laser optics factory in Shenzhen, China; and it also formed a partnership with China's Shenzhen Advanced Science and Technology Development Company to produce cassettes for it in the 1980s. The output was to be used for the Chinese market as well as various world markets. By the end of 1989, Philips had increased its dependence on this plant and had begun manufacturing CD boomboxes, laserdisc players and optical discs. This 50-50 joint venture with Shenzhen used Philips' equipment, worth $40 million, and employees and technicians trained by Philips. In 2001, Philips reduced its share in the joint venture; but by this time, its Chinese partner had had ample opportunity to acquire knowledge of Philips' technology. Philips also had a 20 percent stake in a VCR and other components production plant in Czechoslovakia. Philips provided this plant with production facilities, know-how, information systems and employee training – all forms of tacit knowledge.

Other divestments include the sale of Philips' 35 percent stake in Matsushita to Matsushita's parent company – which by then had learned most of Philips' technologies and product development capabilities in CE products; the sale of its manufacturing division in South Korea to South Korean investors; and the sale of plants that were manufacturing television and audio equipment in Singapore and Brazil in 1998. In 2002, Philips sold its contract-manufacturing unit for CE goods (PCMS, set up by Philips in 1999) to U.S.-based electronics manufacturing services (EMS) company Jabil Circuit, Inc. Under this pact, Philips guaranteed sales worth $4 billion to Jabil over a period of four years, even after the unit was sold. Jabil also acquired nine of Philips' plants (mostly in low-cost locations worldwide) and 5000 employees, including 150 design engineers.

1997 was a landmark year for Philips: after suffering a loss of $349 million in 1996, it undertook a series of measures to boost profits, including a host of outsourcing deals. Its executive vice president and chief financial officer said: "In the past, we did not 'contain our creativity.' Under the label of freedom, we were still spending an enormous amount of money on R&D."[6] This statement indicates the direction of Philips' new outsourcing strategies, through which it gradually reduced its R&D expenditure. In October 1997, Philips ceased in-house production of 19–20-inch television tubes and began sourcing them from Samsung and Toshiba. That same year, it sold its television plant in Greeneville, Tennessee, in the United States to Taylor-White. In 2001, Philips laid off employees at its own VCR factory in Austria and moved production of VCRs to Japan's Funai Electric. Philips gradually reduced its R&D function for CE products and ultimately lost its technological capabilities (discussed below).

Like its American and European competitors before it, Sony also eventually gave in to pressure and increased its reliance on outside operators, gradually moving toward outsourcing deals with foreign firms. Some of Sony's first outsourcing ventures were with domestic companies that it was familiar with. For example, audio speaker manufacturing subsidiary Audio Research was launched in 1969 as a joint venture between Sony and Pioneer, but Sony acquired it in 1972. In 1983, it sold Audio Research in Japan to Minebea, a Japanese producer of ball bearings. Nevertheless,

---

6   "Grundig Charges Push Philips Back into Red," *TV Digest*, February 17, 1997, pp. 12–13.

Sony maintained ties with Audio Research in the form of an outsourcing relationship whereby Sony remained its customer and provided it with R&D support. The alliance constituted a typical Japanese-style *keiretsu* relationship.

Sony also entered into agreements with many different firms in low-cost countries to supply components. By 2000, Sony was outsourcing 60–70 percent of its radio and speakers manufacturing and around 50 percent of its component stereos to Chinese equipment makers. The company claimed that outsourcing to Asian countries such as China and Taiwan would boost its competitiveness against Western firms.

Sony went on to increase outsourcing to other firms such as U.S.-based personal computers and telecommunications equipment manufacturer Solectron. Under this pact, established in 2000, Solectron acquired two of Sony's manufacturing units – one in Japan and the other in Taiwan. Solectron was to retain the employees at the factories and supply products to Sony as well as to other customers. Solectron had been expanding through mergers and had previously acquired Singapore's NatSteel Electronics for $2.4 billion in anticipation of catering to Japanese business.[7] By outsourcing production, Sony hoped to lower costs and increase profitability.

Thenceforth, Sony continued to divest its manufacturing operations in an attempt to reduce fixed investment. Sony even considered outsourcing its core CE production to Aiwa, which was 50 percent owned by Sony at the time. In relation to the decision to outsource production to third parties, Sony's president was reported as saying: "There will be some products on which we think it better to entrust the production also to non-Sony group companies and business partners, and we currently outsource some audio products."[8] Sony outsourced some manufacturing to Celestica, Flextronics and SCI Systems in response to a fall in profits in 1999. By March 2003, Sony had reduced the number of factories worldwide from 70 (in 1999) to 54. Sony hoped that by outsourcing, it could reduce

---

[7]   "Ready to Turn the Key: Asia's Contract Manufacturers are Poised for Japanese Hand-offs," *Electronic Business Asia*, May 2001, http://www.eb-asia.com/EBA/issues/0105/0105c-story.htm.

[8]   "Sony May Sell More Production Plants after Solectron Deal," *AFX News*, October 18, 2000.

the fixed costs of manufacturing by transferring it to other contractor firms and instead concentrate more on the design and planning stages of production. Sony intended to increase its reliance on products from Taiwanese vendors to $938 million by 2001.

Thus, Stage 2 was marked by significant divestitures by the three firms, some of which were to local partners in foreign locations. This enabled the firms to reduce fixed costs, but also gradually pushed the firms into Stage 3 of our model. As outsourcing appeared to produce short-term benefits, they increased their reliance on foreign firms and were soon exposed to the long-term effects of outsourcing.

Stage 3: increased dependence on foreign suppliers

In 1973, NUC sold the Emerson Radio brand name to U.S.-based Major Electronics. Major used to produce radios, tape recorders and other equipment itself; but in 1968, it began importing these products from overseas establishments and became a distributor of finished Far Eastern goods. When it took over Emerson Radio, it was buying 80 percent of its components and products from East Asia. In 1980, Emerson Radio dropped its last U.S.-made product – the phonograph line – because labor costs had made it unprofitable. Thus, Emerson was completely dependent on foreign suppliers for all its finished products. As firm president Stephen Lane commented: "I think most of the profits we've made have been because of controlling overhead and purchasing." According to Lane:

> Our philosophy is simple, that is, to have the best of two worlds. To be in sophisticated, state-of-the-art products by maintaining our own engineering and design capabilities here and keeping close tabs on quality control at all our vendors, and at the same time being able to react quickly to changes by having no hard assets, which would mean worrying about keeping factories going and people employed in a recession.

Other than manufacturing capabilities, Emerson Radio also lost its design and technical capabilities, as it made its fortune by persuading its East Asian suppliers to imitate high-end, branded (Sony, Panasonic) CE products and selling them to consumers at much lower prices. Based on published records, around the mid-1980s, Emerson Radio had outsourcing deals with over 15 Asian suppliers, which depended on Emerson for more than 90 percent of their business. In November 1984, Lane claimed:

"It's been 12 years since we achieved our running goal of 5% net of sales." About this time, Emerson possessed design and engineering capabilities only for audio products. "But, in the video area, outside of the cabinetry, the U.S. firm [had] deferred to the superior design skills of its Japanese suppliers, such as Mitsubishi."[9]

Emerson struggled to hang on to its CE business. In 1985, it acquired CE company H. H. Scott, a relatively small producer of audio equipment; in 1986, it introduced Asian-made refrigerators to the market; and in the following years, it added several more electronics-related products to its range, including computers in 1990. However, by 1991, it had withdrawn the H. H. Scott line and some other CE products. In the late 1980s, having lost its CE capabilities, it had begun diversifying into other areas. By the early 1990s, Emerson Radio was heavily in debt to the tune of over $200 million and was also involved in lawsuits. In 1993, the company finally filed for bankruptcy. What remains of the old Emerson Radio is its brand name – even today, the company capitalizes on the brand by licensing it to other CE firms.

Philips also experienced its own share of troubles due to increased outsourcing. In 1988, Philips' woes reflected those of the U.S. CE firms not too long ago. Its income fell again, which the company blamed on competition from the Far East. As Philips established plants abroad and outsourced production, it gradually increased its dependence on these foreign suppliers and unintentionally but invariably passed on tacit knowledge. The Philips-Sony liaison was a particularly interesting one. It began in October 1979, when the two companies joined forces to use each other's patent rights for certain products (e.g., tapes, cassettes, discs). The pact gave Sony access to Philips' V2000 system and its CD-audio system. Industry analysts concluded that due to this arrangement, Sony learned how to manufacture its own optical videodisc for consumer use, although the company denied these charges. Meanwhile, Philips had plans to launch videodiscs in Europe by 1980. Philips made consumer versions while Sony made industrial videodiscs until 1982, when it announced that it would sell its videodisc production facility in Knoxville, Tennessee – the hometown of NAP.

---

[9]   "Every Which Way is Up for Emerson," *Financial World*, November 14–27, 1984, pp. 86–87.

Philips continued to post lower income forecasts toward the end of the 1980s and planned to cut its workforce by 10 000–20 000 globally in the following years. The company hoped that these initial cost-cutting measures would increase profitability. But in 1988, Philips lowered its forecast for the year and announced that it would be taking more severe measures to improve its operations through further cost cutting. In response to a fall in earnings, the company reduced its European plants from 170 to 110 over the next five years and shifted more production to Mexico and Taiwan. The company was already operating in these countries at the time and this shift increased its reliance on the foreign plants. It hoped these efforts would help it cut costs by $400 million; and profitability did indeed improve for a while, but only temporarily. By the late 1990s, Philips was looking for buyers for its television assembly plant in Juarez, Mexico.

In the late 1980s, Philips was involved in R&D of liquid crystal displays (LCDs) through a joint project between four divisions: consumer electronics, lighting, research and components. While some of the R&D took place at Philips' headquarters in Eindhoven, the Netherlands, production was shifted to the Philips-owned Marantz plant in Japan. In 1986, Philips reorganized Marantz Japan into an R&D base. Prior to 1988, NAP outsourced production of televisions to Matsushita, but in 1988 Marantz Japan Inc (MJI) began shipping VCRs to the United States for sale under the Philips brand. Also in 1988, Philips began manufacturing LCD televisions at the Marantz plant; and it increased its reliance on the manufacturing facility by commencing production of wireless radio equipment there in 1991 and new CD players in 1999. In 1997, Marantz introduced its own (Marantz-branded) low-price version (with some small changes) of Philips' television models in Asia. Hence, Marantz – which was 50.6 percent owned by Philips at the time – had learned Philips' technology, upgraded its competences and forward integrated into launching and marketing its own line of similar products. Finally, in 2001, Philips reduced its controlling ownership stake in MJI, which also acquired the Marantz brand and its business in Europe and the United States from Philips and established its own units in those regions. The two companies still maintained working relations in many areas, but MJI also developed and introduced its own products (mainly audio equipment) under its own brand name, Marantz. A year later, in 2002, Philips further reduced its stake to 14.7 percent in MJI when MJI merged with U.S.-based Denon Ltd.

The late 1990s saw the emergence of digital versatile disc (DVD) technology in the CE industry and in theory, Philips should have been a formidable contender. But by his own admission, Philips' sound and vision chairman and CEO said, with respect to Philips' DVD program in the United States: "We've had to catch up on DVD in every sense of the word. We didn't have a DVD program 12 months ago and now we've launched a player."[10] The company launched a DVD player that was sourced from Toshiba (Japan). By the end of the twentieth century, Philips was on its way out of the CE industry, having lost most of its development capabilities.

Meanwhile, Japan's Sony faced its own set of challenges with its partners. Even after selling its audio speaker manufacturing subsidiary Audio Research to Minebea in 1983 (outlined above), Sony maintained ties with Audio Research in the form of an outsourcing relationship whereby Sony continued to be its customer and to provide it with R&D support. The following year, Minebea set up its own subsidiary for audio R&D by merging Audio Research (acquired from Sony) with another of its divisions, Minebea Denshi Co., Ltd. In this manner, Minebea learned Sony's audio research capabilities.

What started off as simple contractual agreements with foreign operators eventually led Sony to increase its reliance on those partners. Agreements also took the form of joint ventures. For example, in 1992, Viettronics Tan Binh – a Vietnam-based local electric appliance maker – entered into a licensing agreement with Sony to produce color televisions and audio players. In 1994, Sony established a joint venture with the same company to manufacture 14-inch and 21-inch Trinitron color televisions and audio products for the Vietnamese market. Thus, with this new venture in 1994, Sony increased its dependence on Viettronics (from licensing to joint venture) to jointly manufacture goods at low cost.

After concluding the Solectron deal in 2000, Sony announced that it would farm out more production to independent manufacturers if need be. It also finalized plans to create engineering, manufacturing and customer services units to cater to its own needs and those of other firms that outsourced production. As Taiwan was a source of low-cost labor,

---

10   "Philips Plans 2 DVD Players for Europe," *TV Digest*, June 30, 1997, pp. 14–15.

Sony increased its reliance on Taiwanese firms to supply its products. In just one year, Sony bought goods worth $2 billion from Taiwan in 2001 – a sevenfold increase on the same figure from 2000. Such was the extent of its increasing reliance on subcontractors.

In February 2003, Sony entered into a contract with Oak Technology to supply decoder chips to Sony, which would replace the integrated circuit chips developed by Sony's in-house facility. To begin with, the decoder chips were to be used in Sony's digital televisions to be sold in Japan, but Oak Tech also planned to supply chips for use in Sony's products sold in Europe and the United States at a later date. Previously, Oak Tech had entered into a similar decoder supply pact with Sony for its personal video recorders in Japan. Oak Tech also supplied chips to other CE companies like Thomson and Daewoo – another example of Sony's ever-growing dependence on external suppliers and the increasing capabilities of such suppliers.

Sony experienced a rude awakening in 2003. Dubbed the "Sony shock," the company incurred a net loss of $927 million in the first three months of the year. Many said that Sony's state reflected that of the Japanese CE industry and of the national economy as a whole. But the unpredictable global environment and the company's activities in the past few years may have exacerbated its performance. Sony had introduced few "new" products in the recent past; and moreover, it was losing its once-feted technological ability to innovate. The company used to "generate huge profit from its vertically integrated business model in which it developed high-performance parts ... on a commercial basis before anyone else and released hit products based on them."[11] However, in the 1990s, its lost much of its technological reputation as, according to Ken Kutaragi – president of Sony Computer Entertainment and a recent addition to the leadership team – "top management chose not to continue investing in technology."[12]

Sony's technological excellence and product creativity were further tarnished by recalls in 1996 of Sony-made lithium-ion batteries used for notebook computers. The Sony batteries were blamed for causing some

---

[11]   "Maverick on Board to Revive Sony," *Nikkei Weekly*, September 16, 2003.
[12]   "Sony to Reform Production Management Model in China," *SinoCast China IT Watch*, October 6, 2003.

Dell and Apple computers to overheat and catch fire. As if to rub salt into Sony's wounds, delays in the production of blue laser diodes – a key component of Blu-ray disc players – forced Sony to postpone the European release of the PlayStation 3 game console from November 2006 to March 2007. The crises at Sony were also attributed to increased outsourcing, as the company farmed out a large part of production of these components to EMS companies.[13]

Stage 4: industry departure or reduction of outsourcing

As time went by, Emerson Radio and Philips lost their positions in the CE industry. Emerson Radio moved through the first three stages of the model so quickly that it did not get a chance to salvage itself and instead sought to diversify into other, sometimes unrelated areas. The Emerson brand was associated solely with CE and, having lost its technological competences, the firm found itself struggling to survive. Philips shifted its focus away from CE to its lighting and other businesses and managed to survive, but not as a significant CE player.

Although Philips was originally founded as a lighting company, it made a very successful transition into CE and maintained a foothold in the industry for several decades. At several points, in response to declining profitability, Philips restructured its organization and altered its strategies. Before the 1970s, Philips changed its strategy from one of local responsiveness to a more global strategy and reduced the number of product lines. When its V2000 home video system failed around 1980, Philips blamed this on a lack of partnerships with other companies to effectively commercialize its technology. In 1996, Philips incurred a loss of $349 million and once again decided to step up outsourcing and increase its reliance on third-party manufacturers. In 2002, Philips planned to increase outsourcing of chip production from 10 percent to 20–30 percent. The company also increased its reliance on products from United Microelectronics Corp. and Singapore-based Chartered Semiconductor Manufacturing. Thus, Philips never reduced outsourcing, but instead increased it. In June 2001, Philips even abandoned its wireless phone manufacturing efforts; and to cut costs, it also reduced its interest in its Chinese R&D plant by transferring control to its Chinese partner,

---

[13]   "Sony's Technological Leadership in Jeopardy," *Nikkei News*, October 7, 2006.

which was to make phones and supply them to Philips for sale under the Philips name. At the dawn of the twenty-first century, Philips was no longer an independent producer in the CE industry. It sold off its remaining CE divisions, including Polygram; and to emphasize its shift out of CE, CEO Cor Boonstra moved Philips' headquarters from Eindhoven to Amsterdam. Today, Philips still markets some CE products but its main focus is on its other divisions, such as lighting and semiconductors.

The only company that is still active in the industry, Sony, has learned the hazards of excessive outsourcing and has gradually reduced its reliance on outsiders for its core products. Although Sony is better known in the CE industry than the semiconductor industry, it uses semiconductors in many of its CE products (e.g., digital cameras, camcorders). In 1998, Sony's profits fell along with those of other Japanese companies in the semiconductor industry, such as Toshiba and Fujitsu. However, the slump was attributed to lower demand for their products. Surprisingly, in 2000, Sony reduced outsourcing for semiconductors by 5 percent and shifted to in-house production of some of its "most wanted" products, like personal computers, camcorders and digital cameras. There is no hard evidence of why Sony took this decision, but the move followed a fall in profits in 1999. In 2000, Sony announced that it would set up a "supervisory company" to manage design, purchasing and manufacturing for several Sony plants. Thus, although Sony has not entirely eliminated its dependence on outsourcing to keep costs under control, it has moved toward in-house production of its popular money-making products. Also, the establishment of a company to monitor production is indicative of a very cautious components strategy. As Sony president Ando said: "Engineering and manufacturing are (some of) Sony's key strengths. That is why key products will be done by our own internal production, not OEM."[14]

The fear of technology falling in the wrong hands also extends to national governments. In 2000, the Japanese government imposed an export control on Sony's PlayStation 2 (PS2) games console. The PS2's 128-bit central microprocessor, developed by Sony and Toshiba, had twice the raw number-crunching power of Intel's most advanced Pentium chip used in professional desktop computers. Coupled with a video camera,

---

[14]   "Sony Sells Factories in Streamlining Move," *Financial Times*, October 19, 2000.

the PS2 could serve as a makeshift missile-guidance system.[15] Then in 2001, Sony sought to outsource the manufacture of the PS2 console to Taiwanese firms that could produce it at low cost. There were two drivers for this outsourcing initiative. The first was Sony's inability to meet demand; while the second was Microsoft's move to outsource the Xbox (a direct competitor to the PS2) to firms in Taiwan. However, the U.S. and Japanese governments asked Sony to keep production and assembly of the console in Japan, to prevent the Taiwanese firms (which were low-cost subcontractors) from learning the DVD application of the console's chip and using it for military purposes. In 2001, Sony also announced that it would not expand the outsourcing of PC production at its plant in China.

Although on the surface, Sony seemed to have evaded the grave dangers of excessive outsourcing by contracting out only "peripheral operations," it still faced the risk of losing its core competences. In May 2002, Sony stressed that it was keeping key technologies in Japan – unlike other Japanese makers, which were throwing away their future due to outsourcing. Sony reacted to its weakening situation by reducing outsourcing of core operations, but it continued to outsource peripheral technologies. Sony did not seek to increase investment in developing technology or to reinstate control over manufacturing operations until the "Sony shock" of 2003 prompted it to take proactive measures to improve its position in the industry. Under the leadership of Kutaragi, it charted a course to restore its status as a technological leader. To this end, it planned to invest $8.6 billion in "electrical equipment and electronics over three years" and to introduce "in-house production and centralized management of key components." Sony also revealed that it would reduce the number of components used to 100 000 parts (a 90 percent decrease) and indicated 20 000 standard parts to be shared by engineers across the company. By doing so, it sought to shorten the lead time for new product development. In late 2005, Sony announced that under the leadership of its first-ever foreign CEO, Howard Stringer, it would cut 10 000 jobs and close 11 of its 65 plants to boost profits at its electronics unit. However, these cuts and closures were not expected to affect jobs and plants in China, its low-cost manufacturing location.

---

[15]   Richard Re, "Playstation2 Detonation: Controlling the Threat of Dual-Use Technologies," *Harvard International Review*, 25(3), 2003: 46–50.

But solving the problem is a much more difficult task than it might at first appear. First, it requires precisely those fixed investments that the firm's business model is no longer based on. Thus, the question is how to fund this reversal and make it consistent with the firm's strategy. Second, Sony has lost much of its ability to produce and engineer its products, and will have to seriously update its competences by training people and obtaining knowledge externally. Both may come at a high price – particularly since the competitive and technological landscapes may have changed substantially in the meantime. The recent rapid growth of Korean giant Samsung – based more on the insourcing of major components through internal development – epitomizes the risk of excessive outsourcing and a subsequent loss of touch with emerging and ever-evolving technologies. Hence, in Stage 4, there is no ideal solution to the problems around competence losses that a firm has accumulated during the first three stages.

Further questions raised by the four-stage model

The four-stage model raises several further questions. One is why a loss of competence would result, as this appears to be inconsistent with perfectly rational managerial decision-making. Several explanations come to mind. One possibility is a lack of foresight, perhaps due to technological or volume uncertainty. Differing estimations of buyers' and suppliers' ability to develop the underlying competences in future could be another. A further possible reason is strategic myopia that makes the short-term consequences of not outsourcing – in the form of higher fixed costs and higher production costs – look worse than the long-term consequences of outsourcing, in the form of a loss of technological prowess. For instance, the more immediate trigger for outsourcing decisions in these cases appeared to be a downturn in business cycles and short-term financial losses. Outsourcing may also be perceived as a response to adverse demand conditions because of its propensity to lower the breakeven point. This could be framed as a "Faustian dilemma": because of immediate pressures to compete in the marketplace, firms must focus and streamline their production activities, but in order to do so, they must "sell their soul" – that is, their core assets and capabilities – which will catch up with them in the long run. Viewed in this way, there is no myopia but simply a lack of strategic choice. This determinism inevitably drives firms toward more outsourcing. A further implication is that causality in the stage model may well run in both directions: poor results may lead to more outsourcing just as more outsourcing may lead to poorer results.

A second question is why the three firms in our case study experienced their outsourcing cycles and resulting competence losses at different points in time. Emerson was first, in roughly the 1950s to 1970s; Philips followed, in roughly the 1970s to 1990s; and Sony was last, in roughly the 1980s to 2000s. Other CE producers from the same Triad regions seemed to experience similar timings. We would suggest that a combination of the cost competitiveness of the home country and the perceived business models and financial incentives of executives were responsible for such differences in timing. Over time, and with the development of their home economies, firms found that their home country could no longer compete with offshore locations because labor costs were too high. This effect may have arisen sooner in the United States than in Europe, partly because European firms were more effective at limiting imports from lower-cost producers. In Japan, it may have arisen later still, in the 1980s. But executives in these countries are also different. In Japan, outsourcing is seen as a problem-solving tool; while in the United States, it tends to be seen as a problem-removal tool.[16] U.S. managers are incentivized to achieve good short-term results, encouraging them to find cost savings through outsourcing, while this is less true for European (especially Germanic) managers and Japanese managers. The latter group are rewarded more for market share growth than for financial results alone. Our earlier quote from the Emerson executive illustrates this point.

A third issue is whether firms necessarily need to go through all stages of the model for competence loss to occur. Although this is ultimately an empirical question, our cases seem to show that all three firms went through the first three stages in more or less chronological fashion. In Stage 4, however, they took different routes: Sony appeared to use a *voice* (active engagement) strategy, while Emerson and Philips preferred an *exit* (passive engagement) strategy.[17] So there were different responses to the loss of competence through outsourcing.

---

[16]   Masaaki Kotabe, "Efficiency vs. Effectiveness Orientation of Global Sourcing Strategy: A Comparison of U.S. and Japanese Multinational Companies," *Academy of Management Executive*, 12(4), 1998: 107–19.

[17]   For further discussion of *exit* versus *voice* strategy, refer to Albert O. Hirschman, *Exit, Voice, and Loyalty: Responses to Decline in Firms, Organizations, and States* (Cambridge, MA: Harvard University Press, 1970).

Conclusions and implications

Outsourcing can be more than a cost-cutting device and can potentially contribute to a firm's competence base.[18] There are, however, circumstances under which outsourcing leads to the destruction of competence. By documenting the experiences of three firms in the CE industry, we have illustrated how such competence destruction through outsourcing takes place and coined this the "vicious outsourcing cycle." Clearly, not all outsourcing processes will adhere to such a cycle. When firms outsource competences that later become important platforms for growth and innovation, the vicious outsourcing cycle may occur. This stands in contrast to the use of outsourcing to obtain new competences, because in our cases supplier competences appear to be less complementary and more overlapping, which generates the possibility of forward integration by suppliers. In such instances, it is important for firms to consider the future value of in-house production rather than merely the present costs of keeping production in-house versus outsourcing it.

For instance, it was evident in the case of Philips that, based on its past R&D capabilities, it should have been able to compete in the DVD market. But due to excessive outsourcing of components and products before the age of the DVD, it "did not have a DVD program" in the U.S. market, as conceded by Philips Sound and Vision chairman and CEO Doug Dunn.[19] Its European DVD launch also proved unsuccessful. One of the main reasons was that Philips' MPEG-2 DVD technology suffered due to the unavailability of software. The future prospects in relation to the availability of content for these players were also bleak. This preempted the introduction of products based on Philips' DVD technology later. Going back to basics proved harder than expected, because regaining its technical abilities involved building plants and incurring other prohibitively high costs. The case of Philips was also unique because the company's own technologies (e.g., V2000 for videos and MPEG-2 for DVDs) found no support in the market and were largely unsuccessful. Firms in this situation have no choice but to buy products from overseas manufacturers in order to remain in the industry.

---

[18]   James Bryan Quinn, "Strategic Outsourcing: Leveraging Knowledge Capabilities," *Sloan Management Review*, 40(3), 1999: 9–21.

[19]   "Philips Plans 2 DVD Players for Europe," *TV Digest*, June 30, 1997, pp. 14–15.

Our research indicates that most CE firms faced a similar choice: either to exit the product line(s) because sales were dropping or to go abroad like their rivals and lower costs. It is unclear as to whether these firms and others lacked foresight. Based on the patterns in our data, it appears that they started off with one decision, which led to an increasing dependence on suppliers, as our model proposes. These firms progressed through the stages of the model as they faced pressure to meet demand, lower prices and so on. This gradual process culminated in an increase in outsourcing relationships and their outcomes. Upon the sale of Philips' Greenville, Tennessee television plant in mid-1997, Dunn said it was "a tough decision, and I don't take any joy in selling or closing down assets."[20]

Firms do not need to go through all stages of the model for its effects to become visible. Sometimes they do not use offshore subsidiaries but instead go straight to outside suppliers from abroad. At one point in time, Emerson Radio considered setting up subsidiaries in nearby Canada and Latin America, but it eventually relied mainly on external Asian suppliers for its components and finished products. Emerson Radio only went through two of the stages of the cycle and progressed much faster than the other two firms. This was probably due to the market it faced in the United States, which was intensely competitive. Philips, on the other hand, appears to have gone through the first three stages and never really got back to being a technological leader in CE. It would be interesting to observe what patterns other CE firms have followed. Furthermore, one might expect firms in other industries, where international competition has emerged later than in CE, to follow a similar pattern at some point in the future.

From a decision-maker's viewpoint, the vicious outsourcing cycle is more than just a cause for caution. It provides executives with an important criterion for future outsourcing decisions: "To what extent does the activity that we are considering outsourcing embody competences that matter for our future growth and innovation potential? And are we sure that the competences contained in this activity are all easily observable?" This criterion need not replace more traditional considerations of cost minimization or those based on comparisons between the firm's current resource stock and that of its potential suppliers; however, it is a useful supplement

---

[20]   "Philips Plans 2 DVD Players for Europe," *TV Digest*, June 30, 1997, pp. 14–15.

to such considerations. In addition to short-term considerations, firms and their executives need to think about long-term variables such as future growth, continued innovation and sustainability of competitive advantage – all three of which are inextricably linked. There is no *a priori* correct answer to the question whether outsourcing is good or bad for the development of competences inside the firm. Its consequences hinge on the circumstances in which outsourcing takes place and how these conditions then change over time.

In technologically intensive industries such as CE, continued innovation is the key to future growth and sustainability of competitive advantage. But in order to innovate, firms need to be able to identify those competences that underlie components and could possibly lead to the development of unanticipated technology or products in the future. This ability is often elusive or is sometimes sacrificed by myopic executives and executives suffering from the Faustian dilemma we discussed earlier. Executives need to tell themselves not to think in terms of "just one more component" to be outsourced. The three firms in our sample had the potential to innovate but they started giving this away bit by bit. This does not mean that firms should necessarily increase their R&D budget or keep all production activities in-house. But it calls for more judicious outsourcing strategies. Some firms have recognized this need – for example, Sony has shifted some of its semiconductor manufacturing back in-house. Semiconductors, which are used in almost all electronics equipment today, are the basis for future innovation and knowledge of the semiconductor manufacturing process should ideally enable Sony to sustain its technological capabilities. Another important step forward seems to be the ability to move on from one type of product to the next. Emerson never really made it beyond the radio and started losing out when it missed out on the DVD revolution. So, firms that outsource need to think about how they can proceed to entirely new products without having productive capacity. That may require different forms of cooperation at the R&D stage – for instance, with specialist manufacturing outsourcing companies such as Flextronics, which unfortunately were not yet around when Emerson and Philips made their decisions.

Summary

This chapter has illustrated the global sourcing strategies employed by three leading global CE companies over time. The implications are consistent with those described in Chapter 4. First, increasing competition at home and from abroad drives the principal firm to reduce costs by moving relatively labor-intensive assembly and manufacturing activities to lower-cost locations for immediate cost benefits. Second, the principal firm further tries to reduce its fixed manufacturing investment in those lower-cost locations by selling it to local firms, which in turn become suppliers (outsourcees) to the principal firm. By doing so, the principal firm can improve its return on investment by outsourcing. Third, the principal firm comes to realize the gradual loss of its current technological knowledge as well as its own manufacturing capabilities by not staying directly involved in those activities. Fourth, the principal company begins to wonder what it can do to stay viable in the industry, if at all. Destiny diverged in the case of the three global CE firms studied in this chapter.

Simply stated, while the short-term benefits of outsourcing are relatively easy to identify and pursue, the long-term implications of excessive outsourcing – prompted by firms' narrow focus on core competency – could come with a fundamental risk of not only gradually losing their current capabilities, but also losing their ability to keep abreast of ever-changing technologies for sustainable competitive advantage.

6   Managing physical distribution[1]

Introduction

Physical distribution is inextricably tied to international trade, multinational manufacturing and sourcing of raw materials, components and supplies. Physical distribution has become considerably more complex and costly, and thus more important for the success of a firm. A variety of factors contribute to the increased complexity and cost of global logistics, as compared to domestic logistics.

Distance

The first fundamental difference is distance. Global logistics frequently involves the transportation of parts, supplies and finished goods over much longer distances than is the norm domestically. Longer distances generally result in higher direct costs of transportation and insurance for damages, deterioration and pilferage in transit, and higher indirect costs for warehousing and inventory.

Exchange rate fluctuations

The second difference pertains to currency variations in international logistics. The corporation must adjust its planning to incorporate the existence of currencies and changes in exchange rates. For example, in the mid-1990s, when the Japanese yen appreciated faster than the U.S. dollar against key European currencies, Honda found it much more economical to ship its Accord models to Europe from its U.S. plant in Marysville, Ohio, rather than from its plants in Japan.

---

[1]   This chapter is derived primarily from my earlier works, including Masaaki Kotabe and Kristiaan Helsen, *Global Marketing Management*, 9th ed. (Hoboken, NJ: Wiley, 2023), Chapter 15.

Foreign intermediaries

Additional intermediaries participate in the global logistics process because of the need to negotiate border regulations and deal with local government officials and distributors. Although home country export agents, brokers and export merchants work as intermediaries providing an exporting service for manufacturing firms, these home-based intermediaries do not necessarily have sufficient knowledge of foreign countries' market conditions or sufficient connections with local government officials and distributors. In Asian countries such as Japan, South Korea and China, personal "connections" of who knows whom frequently seem to outweigh the Western economic principle of profit maximization or cost minimization when conducting business.[2] Therefore, working with local distributors has proved very important in building initial connections with the local business community as well as local government regulators.

Regulation

The bulk of international trade is handled through ocean shipping. Because the United States is the world's largest single trading country in terms of both exports and imports, and most of its trading partners are located across the Pacific and the Atlantic Oceans, U.S. regulations on ocean transport services directly affect foreign exporters to the United States (as well as U.S. importers of foreign goods) in terms of shipping costs and delivery time. In the United States, the Merchant Marine Act of 1920 (also known as the Jones Act) forbids foreign-owned freighters from transporting passengers and merchandise from one U.S. domestic port to another by restricting foreign access to the domestic shipping market. The Act requires passengers and merchandise being transported by ship within the United States to travel on U.S.-built, U.S.-owned and U.S.-staffed vessels, while allowing unilateral retaliatory action against restrictions imposed by other countries. In March 2003, more than 50

---

[2]   See, for example, Jean L. Johnson, Tomoaki Sakano and Naoto Onzo, "Behavioral Relations in Across-Culture Distribution Systems: Influence, Control, and Conflict in U.S.-Japanese Marketing Channels," *Journal of International Business Studies*, 21, Fourth Quarter 1990: 639–55; Chris Rowley, John Benson and Malcolm Warner, "Toward an Asian Model of Human Resource Management?: A Comparative Analysis of China, Japan and South Korea," *International Journal of Human Resource Management*, 15, June/August 2004: 917–33.

nations – including Australia, Canada, China, the EU and Japan – filed a joint statement with the World Trade Organization (WTO) calling for the liberalization of international marine transport services during the WTO's new round of multilateral trade negotiations. Until resolved by the WTO, the barriers imposed by the Merchant Marine Act continue to add to the costs of logistics in and around the United States.[3]

Security

Security was not an acutely serious concern until September 11, 2001, when the terrorist attacks in the United States awakened the world to the importance of domestic and international security measures. Transportation costs for exporters have increased because of the extra security measures that shipping lines and terminal operators face.[4] However, if government-imposed user fees or carrier surcharges are too high or come without sufficient advance notice, some exporters could even lose their overseas markets due to increased shipping costs and insurance premiums.

Modes of transportation

The global logistics manager must understand the specific properties of the different modes of transportation in order to use them optimally. The three most important factors in determining the optimal mode of transportation are the value-to-volume ratio, the perishability of the product and the cost of transportation. The value-to-volume ratio is determined by how much value is added to the materials used in the product. The perishability of the product relates to quality degradation over time and/or product obsolescence along the product lifecycle. The cost of transportation should be considered in light of the value-to-volume and perishability of the product.

---

[3]   Robert Spich and Robert Grosse, "How Does Homeland Security Affect U.S. Firms' International Competitiveness?" *Journal of International Management,* 11, December 2005: 457–78.
[4]   Robert Spich and Robert Grosse, "How Does Homeland Security Affect U.S. Firms' International Competitiveness?" *Journal of International Management,* 11, December 2005: 457–78.

Ocean shipping

Ocean shipping encompasses three options. Liner service offers regularly scheduled passage on established routes; bulk shipping normally provides contractual services for specified periods; and the third category is irregular runs. Container ships carry standardized containers that greatly facilitate the loading and unloading of cargo and the intermodal transfer of cargo. Ocean shipping is used extensively for the transport of heavy, bulky or nonperishable products, including crude oil, steel and automobiles. Over the years, shipping rates have been falling as a result of a price war among shipping lines. For example, the average rate for shipping a 20-foot container from China to the West Coast of the United States fell, on average, from $4000 in 1992 to $3000 by 2023.[5] Although most manufacturers rely on existing international ocean carriers, some large exporting companies – such as Honda and Hyundai – have their own fleets of cargo ships. For example, Japanese automobile manufacturer Honda owns its own fleet of cargo ships not only to export its Japan-made cars to North America on its eastbound journey, but also to ship U.S.-grown soybeans back to Japan on its westbound journey. This strategy is designed to increase the vessels' capacity utilization.[6] Indeed, Honda even operates a number of highly successful specialty tofu restaurants in Tokyo frequented by young Japanese trendsetters.[7]

Airfreight

Shipping goods by air has proliferated over the last 50 years. Although the total volume of international trade using air shipping remains quite small – it still constitutes less than 2 percent of international trade in goods – it accounts for more than 20 percent of the value of goods shipped in international commerce. High-value goods are more likely to be shipped

---

[5]   United States Department of Commerce, *Assess Costs Everywhere*, http://acetool.commerce.gov/shipping; "Ship Container from China to United States," *BR*, www.brlogistics.net.

[6]   "Engineers Rule," *Forbes*, September 4, 2006, pp. 112–16; "Honda Mixes Soybeans and Carmaking in U.S.," *New York Times*, April 19, 2005, www.nytimes.com/2005/04/18/business/worldbusiness/18iht–honda.html?_r=0. In 2013, Honda sold its soybean division to Kanematsu, but Honda's fleet of cargo ships continue to be used for westbound shipping of soybeans from the United States.

[7]   The author's personal knowledge.

by air, especially if they have a high value-to-volume ratio. Typical examples include semiconductor chips, liquid crystal display screens and diamonds. Perishable products such as produce and flowers also tend to be airfreighted. Changes in aircraft design have enabled the air transshipment of relatively bulky products. Half a century ago, a large propeller aircraft could hold only 10 tons of cargo. Today's jumbo cargo jets carry more than 30 tons; and medium- to long-haul transport aircraft (e.g., the Boeing 747 Dreamlifter and the Airbus Beluga) can carry more than 100 tons of cargo. These super-sized transport aircraft have facilitated the growth of global courier services such as FedEx, UPS and DHL. Of all regions, Asia-Pacific is the most popular airfreight market today. Asia has become the world's factory floor for the outsourced manufacture of goods and services. The top five commodities moving from Asia-Pacific to the United States are office equipment and computers, apparel, telecoms equipment, electrical machinery and miscellaneous manufactured products. Westbound (from the United States to Asia-Pacific) commodities mainly include documents and small packages, electrical machinery and fruit and vegetables.

Intermodal transportation

More than one mode of transportation is usually employed. Ocean shipping is often the primary transportation mode for shipments; once on land, they can be further shipped by truck, barge, railroad or air. Even if countries are contiguous – such as Canada, the United States and Mexico – various domestic regulations prohibit the unrestricted use of the same trucks between and across national boundaries. When different modes of transportation are involved, or even when shipments are transferred from one truck to another at the national border, it is important to ensure that cargo space is utilized at full load to minimize the per-unit transportation cost.

Trade barriers, customs problems and paperwork slow down logistics cycle times across national boundaries. Although this is true, the recent formation of regional trading blocs – such as the EU, the United States-Mexico-Canada Agreement (USMCA) and the Southern Cone Common Market (MERCOSUR) – is also encouraging the integration and consolidation of logistics in various regions for improved economic efficiency and competition.

Organizing shipments so that they arrive in time at the desired destination is critical in modern-day logistics management. Due to low transit times, greater ease of unloading and distribution and higher predictability, many firms use airfreight – either on a regular basis or as a backup to fill in when a regular ocean shipment is delayed. For footwear firms Reebok and Nike and fashion firms such as Pierre Cardin, the use of airfreight is becoming almost a required way of doing business, as firms jostle to get their products first into the U.S. market from their production centers in Asia and Europe. The customer in a retail store often buys a product that may have been airfreighted in from the opposite end of the world the previous day or even the same day. Thus, the face of retail is also changing as a result of advances in global logistics. The distance between the transacting parties increases transportation costs and requires longer-term commitment to forecasts and longer lead times. Differing legal and traffic environments, liability regimes and pricing regulations affect transportation costs and distribution costs in a way that is not seen in the domestic market.

Warehousing and inventory management

A firm's international strategy for logistics management depends, in part, on government policy and on the infrastructure and logistic services environment. Traditional logistics strategy involves anticipatory demand management based on forecasting and inventory speculation.[8] With this strategy, a multinational firm estimates its requirements for supplies and demand from its customers and then attempts to manage the flow of raw materials and components in its worldwide manufacturing system and the flow of finished products to customers in a way that minimizes holding inventory without jeopardizing manufacturing runs and without losing sales due to stockouts.

In the past, the mechanics and reliability of transportation and tracking of the flow of goods presented major problems. With the increasing use of information technology, electronic data interchange and intermodal transportation, the production, scheduling and delivery of goods across

---

[8]   Louis P. Bucklin, "Postponement, Speculation and the Structure of Distribution Channels," *Journal of Marketing Research,* 2, February 1965: 26–31.

national borders have increasingly become a matter of just-in-time delivery, although some structural problems still remain. For instance, current restrictions on U.S.-Mexico cross-border trucking restrain the speed of goods flow and add to lead times, and are examples of government restrictions that need to be changed to facilitate the faster movement of goods across borders.[9]

Hedging against inflation and exchange rate fluctuations

Multinationals can also use inventory as a strategic tool to deal with currency fluctuations and to hedge against inflation. By increasing inventories before imminent depreciation of a currency instead of holding cash, a firm can reduce its exposure to currency depreciation losses. Large inventories also provide a hedge against inflation because the value of the goods/parts held in inventory remains the same compared to the buying power of the local currency, which falls with a devaluation. In such cases, the international logistics manager must coordinate operations with the rest of the firm so that the cost of maintaining an increased level of inventory is more than offset by the gains from hedging against inflation and currency fluctuations. Many countries, for instance, charge a property tax on stored goods. If the increase in the cost of carrying the increased inventory along with the taxes exceeds the saving from hedging, increased inventory may not be a good idea.

Benefiting from tax differences

Costs can be written off before taxes in creative ways so that internal transit arrangements can actually make a profit. This implies that what and how much a firm transfers within its global manufacturing system is a function of the tax systems in various countries to and from which the transfers are being made. If the transfer of component X from country A to country B is tax deductible in country C (as an export) and gets credit in country D for being part of locally assembled good Y, the transfer makes a profit for the multinational. Access to and use of such knowledge

---

9   Klint W. Alexander and Bryan J. Soukup, "Obama's First Trade War: The US-Mexico Cross-Border Trucking Dispute and the Implications of Strategic Cross-Sector Retaliation on U.S. Compliance Under NAFTA," *Berkeley Journal of International Law*, 28(2), 2010: 313–42.

is the *métier* of logistics firms, which sell these services to multinationals that are keen to optimize their global logistics.

Logistical integration and rationalization

Logistical integration involves coordinating production and distribution across geographical boundaries – a radical departure from the traditional country-by-country-based structure consisting of separate sales, production, warehousing and distribution organizations in each country. Rationalization, on the other hand, involves reducing resources to achieve more efficient and cost-effective operations. Although these are conceptually separate, most companies' logistics strategies include both aspects.

For example, UPS has played a leading role in utilizing technology to create efficiencies for customers. Its use of a cloud-based online platform allows for streamlining among shippers and their international suppliers. With its cloud-based technology, UPS not only has greater control over orders but also can access near real-time data. UPS also uses over 3000 vehicles that are electric, hybrid or fueled by compressed natural gas, propane or liquefied natural gas to lower its emissions around the world. It also helps specific customers to reduce their carbon footprints by employing multimodal networks and alternative forms of transportation. For example, rock band Pearl Jam use UPS to move their gear around for concerts. UPS uses rail as an alternative to traditional touring semitrucks. This reduces the band's carbon footprint, which furthers the band's commitment to sustainability and the environment. UPS has also helped automate the shipping systems of Martin Guitars and has assisted the guitar manufacturer in redesigning its shipping boxes for maximum efficiency.[10]

Dramatic economic integration is taking place across the expanded EU. However, a word of caution is in order. Although EU laws point toward further economic integration, there still are – and will continue to be – political, cultural and legal differences among countries as well. Similarly, the USMCA is not free of arcane regulations. For example, "cabotage" refers to the right of a trucker to carry goods in an assigned territory. Traditionally, countries have restricted the cabotage rights of foreign truckers. If a U.S. trucking company has a scheduled load to the United

---

[10]   "UPS Logistics a Masterpiece of Streamlined Supply Chain Management," www.supplychain247.com, August 20, 2013; www.UPS.com.

States from Toronto, Canada, the truck may carry the load but the driver must be Canadian. Similarly, a U.S. trucker, having delivered goods in Toronto, cannot pick up another load and deliver it in Ottawa, another city in Canada – that would be a violation of current cabotage rules. Even under the USMCA, Canada, the United States and Mexico have varying – and even sometimes confusing – regulations on cabotage rights.

Consequently, despite the promised benefit of logistics integration and rationalization, supply chain managers and corporate planners must have specialized local knowledge to ensure smooth operations. Customer service strategies in particular need to be differentiated, depending on the expectations of local consumers. For example, German buyers of personal computers (PCs) may be willing to accept Dell Computer's mail order service or its website ordering service, but French and Spanish customers will assume that a delivery person will deliver and install the products for them.

E-commerce and logistics

Another profound change in the last two decades has been the proliferation of the internet and e-commerce. The internet opened the gates for companies to sell easily and directly to consumers across national boundaries. Manufacturers that traditionally sell through the retail channel can benefit most from e-commerce. Furthermore, customer information is no longer held hostage by the retail channel.

We emphasize "can" because, in reality, logistics is not as easily globalized as e-commerce. This revolutionary way of marketing products around the world was originally epitomized by Dell Computer, which put pressure on the industry's traditional players with a simple concept: sell PCs directly online to customers, with no complicated channels. Michael Dell successfully introduced a new way for PC companies to compete – not by technology alone, but by emphasizing customers' needs and satisfying them quickly and efficiently, and above and beyond traditional national boundaries. Major PC companies are now compressing the supply chain via concepts such as "build to order" rather than "build to forecast." However, while order taking can take place globally, shipping of PCs must be local or regional, for various reasons.

You may ask why most e-businesses do not ship overseas if the internet makes any company instantly global. In addition, why do more companies not make their internet-powered supply chains globally accessible? The answer is that it remains very difficult to manage the complex logistics, financial, linguistic and regulatory requirements of global trade. E-businesses operating from one central location also cannot address logistical problems associated with local competition and exchange rate fluctuations. For example, Australia's largest bookseller, Dymocks, offers just over 100 000 books online. This Australian company is no comparison in size to Amazon. However, it does have a competitive advantage over Amazon: a comprehensive offering of books published in Australia. Furthermore, competing on price for international sales without local distribution is tricky, as exchange rates fluctuate. When the Australian dollar depreciated during the Asian financial crisis, buying from Amazon and other U.S. online retailers became more expensive in Australia. Australian consumers logged on to local alternatives such as dymocks.com instead. As a result, leading e-commerce sites now offer regional websites to handle sales in various parts of the world. For example, Amazon now has 20 regional websites[11] around the globe to accommodate regional and local differences.

Another example is Compaq Computer (later acquired by Hewlett-Packard) in Latin America. In the early 2000s, the company was extremely successful at selling computers online throughout Latin America. The company guaranteed delivery within 72 hours of placing orders. Latin Americans shopping online could buy the computers in the local currency and did not have to bring them through customs. This required local assembly of Compaq computers. Compaq had assembly plants in Mexico, Ecuador, Argentina, Brazil, Venezuela, Chile, Puerto Rico, Colombia and Peru.[12]

The web may have dispensed with physical stores, but local adaptation of product offerings and the establishment of local distribution centers

---

[11]   Australia, Brazil, Canada, China, Egypt, France, Germany, India, Italy, Japan, Mexico, Netherlands, Poland, Saudi Arabia, Singapore, Spain, Sweden, Turkey, the United Arab Emirates and the United Kingdom.
[12]   "IT Watch," *Business Latin America*, September 13, 1999, p. 7; "Latin American PC Market Continues to Grow," *World IT Report*, February 19, 2002, p. N.

remain as crucial as ever. Local competition has forced Amazon and other American e-commerce companies to reassess what it means to operate globally on the internet.

Third-party logistics management

Good logistics can make all the difference in a company's ability to serve its customers. The crucial factor is not just what the company makes or how the product is made; it is also how quickly the company can get the parts together or shift finished products from its factories to markets. Despite the immense competitive advantage that logistics can generate for the organization, manufacturers often find that logistics operations are usually faster and less expensive if they are outsourced and organized by specialists and professionals, known as third-party logistics providers (3PLs), which have competence in integrated logistics management and the ability to service multiple clients and products.

Although logistics management handled by 3PLs may not be visible to ordinary consumers, the significance of 3PL operations in today's logistics management behind the scenes is evident from the statistics. For example, while Amazon had increased its ownership of warehouse and distribution space to 22 million square feet around the world by the end of 2022, this is dwarfed by one major U.S.-based 3PL company, Prologis, which controls roughly 1 billion square feet of warehouses and distribution centers used by major clients including Amazon, Home Depot and FedEx.[13] In fact, 90 percent of Fortune 500 companies operating in the United States now seek assistance from one or more 3PLs. Shippers need 3PLs for outsourcing, which brings down costs and improves efficiency. 3PLs are very effective at handling e-commerce needs in the business-to-consumer market. Another value of 3PLs is that many larger providers have numerous warehouses and fulfillment centers scattered across the United States where they can draw on stock at the nearest customer location. International

---

[13] "Amazon Buying Its Own Warehouse Space: Will That Hurt Industrial REITs?" *Yahoo!Finance*, https://shorturl.at/fjn25, February 14, 2023; "Warehouse Giant Prologis, A Major Amazon Landlord, to Buy Rival Duke Realty in $26 Billion Deal," *CNBC.com*, https://shorturl.at/iktu3, June 13, 2022.

shipments for retailers using 3PLs can be cheaper and more effective, as the responsibility is transferred to the shipper.[14]

However, a company needs a close working relationship with several 3PLs to avoid a catastrophe similar to that experienced by Kentucky Fried Chicken (KFC) in England in early 2018, which provides insight into supply chain vulnerabilities that all organizations should note. Two-thirds of KFC's 900 U.K. locations were affected by a breakdown in the supply chain, leading to shortages of chicken, gravy and other items. KFC's parent company, Yum Brands, reported that the supply chain problem would negatively affect earnings. The breakdown of KFC's supply chain occurred when it switched from a specialty food distributor to a mega-freight forwarder. This mega-freight forwarder, like many 3PLs, relied on a complicated patchwork of individual trucking companies and other carriers to deliver the goods. Companies should work closely with the 3PLs they use to keep track of which carriers will be used for their shipments, ensuring that quality is cascaded down to the subcontractors within the 3PLs they have engaged.[15]

Interestingly, as more companies resort to 3PLs, express operators are moving into a broader range of logistics businesses. In the United States, one service offered by local branches of UPS is a drop-off facility for broken Toshiba laptops. Most laptop owners think that when they tell Toshiba about their problem and put their laptop into a UPS box, it is sent to the Japanese company for repair and then returned by UPS. But what really happens is that when the laptop arrives at UPS's Louisville hub, it is taken to a vast estate of warehouses near the airport and mended in a repair shop owned and run not by Toshiba, but by UPS. The UPS technicians are trained by Toshiba and the warehouse holds Toshiba spare parts. Even the people in the Toshiba call center that deal with inquiries work for UPS. The delivery company has been contracted to provide a complete repair and customer service operation. This partnership with UPS played a key role in Toshiba winning back market share in 2010 to

[14]   "Fortune 500 Companies are Using 3PLs More, Study Finds," *Supplychaindive*, https://shorturl.at/glzHS, May 30, 2017.

[15]   "Top 50 US and Global Third Party Logistics Providers (3PL) in 2017: Collaboration is Now Paramount," *Logistics Management*, https://www .logisticsmgmt.com/article/top_50_us_and_global_third_party_logistics _providers_3pl_in_2017_collaborat, June 6, 2018.

become the fourth-largest player in the U.S. laptop market. Having done this for one company, UPS could then capitalize on its investment by providing a similar service to others.[16]

The recent COVID-19 pandemic heightened the trend of businesses outsourcing their logistics to 3PL partners. More than ever, companies are looking to outsource not just basic operations but also design, planning and other logistics services to 3PLs.[17]

A word of caution is in order, however. Despite the potential benefits for both the company and customers, 3PL sourcing also comes with risks. These risks (as well as the benefits) can be classified as strategy, finance and operation related. Strategy-related risks may include loss of control over the logistics function, the leakage of sensitive information and the loss of customer contact, to name a few. In the finance-related domain, the risks of 3PL outsourcing can range from unrealistic fee structures and financial losses to cost-saving assessment difficulties. Operational-related risks include poor IT capabilities, personnel quality and customer service; inadequate expertise; and an inability to handle special product needs.[18]

The internet and the logistics revolution

The 3PL trend resulted from the proliferation of both the internet and intranets (specialized secure internet channels established between and within companies), as well as a greater concentration on core competencies. The internet and intranets facilitate on-time inventory and distribution coordination without the constraints of geographical boundaries. "Core competencies" are the mix of skills and resources that a firm possesses that enable it to produce one set of goods and/or services in

---

[16] "Partnership with UPS Enabled Toshiba to Speed Up Laptop Repair Service," *Business Today*, https://www.businesstoday.in/magazine/cover-story/story/innovation-toshiba-ups-25174-2011-11-22, December 11, 2011.

[17] "Logistics Outsourcing Will Increase Throughout 2020," *Redwood Logistics*, https://shorturl.at/akILX, July 14, 2020.

[18] Kostas Selviaridis, Martin Spring, Vassilios Profillidis and George N. Botzoris, "Benefits, Risks, Selection Criteria and Success Factors for Third-Party Logistics Services," *Maritime Economics & Logistics*, 104, 2008: 380–92.

a much more effective manner than other firms. In addition, competent logistics firms can save money for multinationals shipping components between their facilities in different countries, because the shipping costs paid internally can vary according to foreign currency fluctuations.

We illustrate how some major companies have taken advantage of the internet and intranets to streamline their logistics. Pharmaceutical giant Eli Lilly has gradually outsourced more of its global logistics to Swiss-based Danzas AEI Intercontinental. The e-logistics company's famed MarketLink system seamlessly manages logistics services driven by the real-time flow of data between the company and its customers. Danzas was recently tasked with handling customs and the delivery of Eli Lilly's airborne and ocean imports. Based in the pharmaceutical hub of Basel, Switzerland, Danzas has increasingly specialized in pharmaceutical products and is also working with GlaxoSmithKline and Hoffmann-La Roche.[19]

As the 3PL market has increased substantially since the 1990s, many traditional shippers – such as UPS, Federal Express, Yamato Transport and DHL – have developed large business units devoted exclusively to integrated logistics. Many logistics companies are now moving to provide tailored logistics solutions in international markets for their clients. One major player is Omnitracs, which is home to industrial engineers, software systems integrators and developers, facility designers, operations managers, high-tech repair technicians, logisticians and transportation, financial, e-commerce and international trade experts. It offers a full spectrum of supply chain services and logistics expertise around the world to improve the productivity, reliability, routing, safety and compliance of clients' transportation assets through its innovative software and unique fleet management solutions.[20]

Even online companies, such as Amazon, increasingly rely on 3PL services in foreign markets. Amazon launched its Canadian website (www.amazon .ca) in July 2002, with logistics handled by Canada Post Corp. In 2001, more than 250 000 Canadians ordered products from Amazon's U.S. site

---

[19]   Robert Koenig, "Danzas Expands Pharmaceutical Logistics Business with Eli Lilly," *Journal of Commerce*, December 7, 1998: 14A; "Danzas AEI Intercontinental," *Journal of Commerce*, November 25, 2002: 32.
[20]   www.omnitracs.com.

and Canada represents Amazon's largest export market. Amazon.ca features bilingual Canadian content and 1.5 million items, with Canada Post handling domestic deliveries. Canada Post subsidiary Assured Logistics handles supply chain services such as warehousing, inventory management and online fulfillment. This has proved to be a mutually beneficial arrangement. Canada Post is establishing itself as a competent player in the online world, and as a result, its business has picked up: about 300 Canadian companies now use its online logistical services. On the other hand, Amazon spends $200 million a year on technology to keep its U.S. operation running but does not incur those costs in its Canadian operation through amazon.ca. Furthermore, this arrangement permits Amazon to better cater to local market needs in Canada.[21]

In China, "*wu lui*" means "the flow of things" – in other words, logistics. Alibaba – China's largest e-commerce firm – has gone one step further, adopting an asset-light approach. Instead of owning its own delivery trucks, it has joined forces with a number of courier firms which have invested RMB 100 billion (about US$15 billion) in developing a smart logistics network relying on big data. These firms analyze customer information so that resources can be deployed more efficiently. Alibaba also has entered into a cooperation pact with China Post. By sharing warehouses, processing centers and delivery personnel, the firm hopes to deliver online purchases within 24 hours even to small cities and villages.[22]

Thanks to the rapid development of IT, a new technology known as the "Internet of Things" (IoT) is revolutionizing the logistics industry. According to research conducted by Zebra Technologies, among 600 manufacturing companies surveyed, 97 percent of respondents believe that IoT is the most significant technology of the decade. The simplest way to think of the IoT is as the networked connection of physical objects. The IoT encompasses a diverse array of different technologies, including wireless (e.g., Bluetooth, RFID and WiFi) and wide area connections (e.g., 4G and LTE), as well as wired connections. IoT benefits can extend across

---

[21] "Amazon Lands in Canada, Outsources Logistics," *Computing Canada*, July 5, 2002, p. 6; "Place an Order for Delivery to a Canada Post Pickup Point," www.amazon.ca/.

[22] "The Flow of Things," *The Economist*, www.economist.com, July 12, 2014.

the entire logistics value chain, including warehousing operations, freight transportation and last-mile delivery.[23]

Another technology that can improve transport management is block-chain. Blockchain technology can work in concert with IoT-based systems to provide shipment data and guarantee information accuracy. Blockchain technology provides better accountability with transportation management providers, systems and contractors. It also eliminates the need for more back-office staff to support transportation management. Carriers have access to information regarding demand, making forecasting more accurate. Lastly, electronic logging device implementation and fleet maintenance are a perfect fit for blockchain use.[24]

Free trade zones

A free trade zone (FTZ) is an area that is located within a nation but is considered outside of the national customs territory. The use of FTZs has become an integral part of global sourcing strategy, as they offer various tax benefits and marketing flexibility on a global basis.

Many countries have similar programs. Today, FTZs employ roughly 90–100 million workers worldwide, including 450 000 in the United States.[25] In the United States, FTZs are officially called "foreign trade zones." FTZs are licensed by the Foreign Trade Zone Board and operate under the supervision of the Customs Service. The level of demand for FTZ procedures has followed the overall growth trend in global trade and investment. In the United States, in 2020, some 200 FTZs had been established, with a total of 347 active production operations. Over 470 000 persons were employed at some 3400 firms to work in FTZs that year. The value of shipments into zones totaled nearly $625 billion in 2020, com-

---

[23] "How the Internet of Things is Transforming Manufacturing Today," www .supplychain247.com, September 9, 2015; "Internet of Things in Logistics," www.dhl.com.

[24] "How Will Blockchain Ledger Technology Impact Shippers?" *Supply Chain*, www.supplychain.com, September 1, 2018.

[25] *U.S. Foreign-Trade Zones: Background and Issues for Congress*, U.S. Congressional Research Service, https://sgp.fas.org/crs/misc/R42686.pdf, December 19, 2019.

pared with over $767 billion in 2019; the drop was due to the outbreak of the COVID-19 pandemic in 2020 (see Figure 6.1).[26] U.S. FTZs account for 10 percent of all foreign goods entering the United States.[27] Companies operating in FTZs can save money, improve cash flow and increase logistical efficiency. Legally, goods in the zone remain in international commerce as long as they are held within the zone or are exported. In other words, those goods (including materials, components and finished products) shipped into a FTZ in the United States from abroad are legally considered as not having landed in the customs territory of the United States and thus are not subject to U.S. import tariffs, as long as they are not sold outside the FTZ in the United States (see Table 6.1).

Source: International Trade Administration, Department of Commerce.

Figure 6.1 Foreign trade zones in the United States

A FTZ provides many cash-flow and operating advantages as well as marketing advantages to users. Even when goods enter the United States,

---

[26] *U.S. Foreign-Trade Zone (FTZ) Program*, U.S. Congressional Research Service, February 26, 2020.

[27] *U.S. Foreign-Trade Zones: Background and Issues for Congress*, U.S. Congressional Research Service, December 19, 2020.

customs duties can be levied on the lesser of the value of the finished product or its imported components.

Table 6.1   Benefits of using a FTZ in the United States

Duty deferral and elimination: Duty will be deferred until the products are sold in the United States. If the products are exported elsewhere, no import tariff will be imposed.

Lower tariff rates: Tariff rates are almost always lower for materials and components than for finished products. If materials and components are shipped to a FTZ for further processing and finished products are sold in the United States, a U.S. import tariff will be assessed on the value of the materials and components, rather than on the value of the finished products.

Lower tariff incidence: Imported materials and components that, through storage or processing, undergo loss or shrinkage may benefit from FTZ status, as tariffs are assessed only on the value of materials and components that actually find their way into the product.

Exchange rate hedging: Currency fluctuations can be hedged against by requesting customs assessment at any time.

Import quotas not applicable: Import quotas are not generally applicable to goods stored in a FTZ.

"Made in the USA" designation: If foreign components are substantially transformed within a FTZ located in the United States, the finished product may be designated as "Made in the USA."

Operationally, a FTZ provides opportunities for businesses engaged in international commerce to take advantage of a variety of efficiencies and economies in the manufacture and marketing of their products. Merchandise within the zone can be unpacked and repacked; sorted and relabeled; inspected and tested; repaired or discarded; reprocessed, fabricated, assembled or otherwise manipulated. It can be combined with other imported or domestic materials; stored or exhibited; transported in bond to another FTZ; sold or exported. Foreign goods can be modified within the FTZ to meet U.S. import standards and can be processed using U.S. labor.

Aging imported wine is an interesting way to take advantage of a FTZ. A U.S. wine importer purchases what is essentially newly fermented grape juice from French vineyards and ships it to a FTZ in the United States for aging. After several years, the now-aged French wine can be shipped throughout the United States, where an appropriate U.S. import tariff is assessed on the original value of the grape juice instead of on the market value of the aged wine. If tariff rates are sufficiently high, the cost savings from using a FTZ can be enormous.

Another effective use of a FTZ is illustrated by companies such as Ford and Dell Computer. These companies rely heavily on imported components such as auto parts and computer chips, respectively. These companies can have part of their manufacturing facilities designated as subzones of a FTZ. They can thus use those facilities as normal, while enjoying all of the benefits accruing from a FTZ. Furthermore, if foreign components are substantially transformed within a FTZ located in the United States, the finished product may be designated as "Made in the USA." To the extent customers have a favorable attitude toward the country of origin, such labeling has an additional marketing advantage.

At the macro level, all parties to the arrangement benefit from the operation of FTZs. The government maintaining the FTZs benefits from increased investment and employment. The firm using the FTZ can establish a beachhead in the foreign market without incurring all costs normally associated with such activity. As a result, goods can be reassembled and large shipments can be broken down into smaller units. Duties may be due only on the imported materials and the component parts rather than on the labor that is used to finish the product.

In recent years, major emerging economies such as China and India have rushed to establish FTZs and special economic areas to facilitate exports and provide employment opportunities. These zones are exempt from certain federal laws regarding taxes, quotas, foreign direct investment and labor, in order to ensure products can be made there at competitive prices. India first allowed FTZs, known as special economic zones, after passing the Special Economic Zones Act on June 23, 2005; while China introduced the Shanghai FTZ in September 29, 2013 as a testing ground for new trade reforms.[28]

---

[28]   "Shanghai Free-Trade Zone: Chinese to Invest Abroad in Free-Trade Zone Trial," *South China Morning Post*, www.scmp.com, April 29, 2015; "China's Free Trade Zones – Where Are They?" China Checkup, www.chinacheckup .com, April 25, 2018; "China's Foreign Investment Law Fails to Address U.S. Concerns," Lawfare, www.lawfareblog.com, March 7, 2019.

For logisticians, the decision on whether to use FTZs is framed by the overall benefit to the logistics system. Clearly, transport and retransport are often required, warehousing facilities must be constructed and material handling frequency increases. However, the costs could well be balanced by preferential government treatment or by lower labor costs.

International distribution channels

Both consumer and industrial products go though some form of distribution process in all countries and markets. International distribution channels are the link between a firm and its customers in markets around the world. For a firm to realize its marketing objectives, it must be able to make its product accessible to its target market at an affordable price. A firm cannot do this if its distribution structures are inflexible, inefficient and burdensome. Creating a reliable and efficient international distribution channel is one of the most critical and challenging tasks that an international marketing manager can face.

Channel configurations

In essence, companies have two options when it comes to configuring their international distribution systems:

- selling directly to customers in a foreign market by using their own local salesforce or through the internet; or
- using the resources of independent intermediaries, most often at the local level.

Australian company ResMed, a manufacturer of medical respiratory devices, is an example of a firm that uses the first option above. Most of ResMed's foreign sales are generated by its own sales staff operations from its own sales offices in the United States, the United Kingdom and throughout Europe and Southeast Asia. Although this direct distribution channel may appear to be the most effective, it will succeed only if customers are geographically homogeneous, have similar consumption patterns and are relatively few in number.[29] Dell and Hewlett-Packard are two examples of multinationals in the same industry with different distribution systems. Dell distributes its PCs directly from its assembly factories to end users all around the world, while Hewlett-Packard uses international agents and retailers. Dell customers may have to wait several days or weeks to get a PC, whereas Hewlett-Packard customers can walk away from a retailer with a PC immediately. In deciding which distribution channel to adopt, a firm must consider the cost of meeting customer needs. Therefore, a firm must evaluate the impact on customer service and cost when comparing different international distribution options.

Distribution channels that position intermediaries, agents or merchants between the manufacturer and customers can often involve several levels and employ several intermediaries, each with its own specific purpose within the distribution channel. The use of intermediaries can be a relatively easy, quick and low-cost strategy to enter a foreign market; therefore, this is a common choice for many companies – particularly small- to medium-sized companies – that do not have the resources to operate their own marketing and distribution system in a foreign market. Figure 6.2 shows some of the distribution channel configurations.

Within a distribution channel, a firm can elect to go through one or more agent or merchant intermediaries. The basic difference between agent and merchant intermediaries concerns the legal ownership of goods. An agent intermediary does not take title (ownership) to the goods; rather, it distributes them on behalf of the principal company in exchange for a percentage of the sale price. Merchant intermediaries hold title to the goods they exchange and operate in their own right as independent businesses. The names given to intermediaries can vary from country to country and from industry to industry in the same country.

Apart from meeting customer needs and costs, several other factors influence the choice of distribution channel configuration used by a firm to gain access to international markets, including the characteristics of customers; the range and choice of intermediaries; competitors; the marketing environment; and the strengths and weaknesses of the company

---

[29]   Bruce Seifert and John Ford, "Export Distribution Channels," *Columbia Journal of World Business*, 24(2), 1989: 15–22.

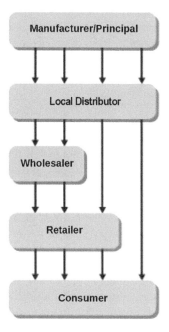

Source: Adapted from Masaaki Kotabe and Kristiaan Helsen, *Global Marketing Management*, 9th ed. (Hoboken, NJ: Wiley, 2023), p. 555.

Figure 6.2   International distribution channel alternatives

itself.[30] These factors stand out as being particularly important in selecting a proper distribution channel in terms of market coverage, control and cost.

"Coverage" refers to the market segments or geographic areas in which a firm's products are represented. Although full market coverage may be the company's ultimate objective, it is not always possible in a foreign market; nor may it be desirable. In some countries, such as China and Brazil, the country's most affluent and viable market segments for foreign products are based in three or four major cities. If a firm wishes to attempt full market coverage, it may have to use several intermediaries.

---

[30]   Bert Rosenbloom and Trina L. Larsen, "International Channels of Distribution and the Role of Comparative Marketing Analysis," *Journal of Global Marketing*, 4(4), 1991: 39–54.

The more intermediaries in the distribution channel, the more likely it is that the firm will lose control over all aspects in the marketing of its products. If a firm wishes to have complete control over aspects of its marketing – such as prices, the types of outlets in which products should be available, inventory levels and promotion – it has little choice but to develop its own company-controlled distribution system.

Although direct distribution may afford a firm complete control over all aspects of the marketing of its products, this comes at significant cost. This is particularly true where the sales base is relatively small. Channel costs include the margins, markups and commissions payable to the various intermediaries. Although these costs may inflate a product's price in a foreign market, companies may be disappointed if they believe they can reduce channel costs by using a direct distribution strategy. Local costs associated with maintaining a salesforce and inventory, providing credit and advertising may offset any cost savings.

Most often, in reality, no one factor is more important than another in configuring an international distribution channel. A channel with optimum coverage and control at minimum cost is the preferred choice; but in practice, a balance must be struck.

Channel management

Use of an indirect distribution channel always results in a loss of some control over the company's marketing operations. This loss of control can be greater in international distribution channels than in domestic ones because the company has no permanent presence in the foreign market and must rely heavily on the actions of its foreign intermediaries. Differences in expectations and goals between the company and its foreign intermediaries can lead to channel conflict. To deal with this, companies must actively manage the relationships between themselves and their intermediaries, and often among intermediaries themselves, in order to build a harmonious relationship characterized by loyalty, trust, cooperation and open communication.[31] In China, for example, it is also

---

[31]   Leonidas C. Leonidou, Constantine S. Katsikeas and John Hadjimarcou, "Building Successful Export Business Relationships: A Behavioral Perspective," *Journal of International Marketing*, 10(3), 2002: 96–115.

important to cultivate political ties with key officials in local government, industry bureaus and state banks, among others.[32]

The selection of intermediaries is crucial both in maintaining harmonious channel relationships and in achieving foreign sales and other marketing objectives. Guidelines for selecting and dealing with foreign intermediaries include the following:[33]

- Search for intermediaries capable of developing markets, not just those with good contacts.
- Regard intermediaries as long-term partners, not as a temporary means of market entry.
- Actively search for and select intermediaries; do not let them select you.
- Support your intermediaries by committing resources such as marketing ideas, funds and know-how.
- Ensure intermediaries provide the information you need, including up-to-date market information and detailed sales performance data.
- Maintain as much control as possible over the marketing strategy.
- Forge links with national intermediaries as soon as possible after entering a foreign market.
- Maintain a genuine interest in both the intermediary and the foreign market.
- Be prepared to adapt to the local competitive conditions.
- Attempt to minimize any disagreements with an intermediary as quickly as possible.

International retailing

The face of distribution that consumers interact with is the retail store at which they shop. In developed parts of the world, retailing employs between 7 and 12 percent of the workforce and wields tremendous power over manufacturers and consumers. "International retailing" is any retail-

---

[32]   Maggie Chuoyan Dong, Caroline Bingxin Li and David K. Tse, "Do Business and Political Ties Differ in Cultivating Marketing Channels for Foreign and Local Firms in China?" *Journal of International Marketing*, 21, March 2013: 39–56; Walter Frick, "In China, Right Political Ties Count," *Harvard Business Review*, 92, November 2014: 30–31.

[33]   David Arnold, "Seven Rules of International Distribution," *Harvard Business Review*, 78, November/December 2000: 131–37.

ing activity that transcends national borders. Over the last two decades, retailers have grown into some of the world's largest companies, rivaling or exceeding manufacturers in terms of global reach. They have grown much faster abroad than in their domestic markets. The international operations of the world's top 10 retailers are summarized in Table 6.2. Due to the size of their home markets, Home Depot and Target in the United States and JD.com in China, respectively, are some of the largest retailers without foreign operations.

Table 6.2   International operations of the world's top 10 retailers in 2021

Rank	Company	Country of origin	2021 net retail revenue (US $ billion)	2016–2021 revenue compound annual growth rate (%)	Number of foreign markets
1	Walmart	United States	572.8	3.3	24
2	Amazon.com	United States	239.2	20.4	21
3	Costco	United States	195.9	10.5	12
4	Schwarz (Lidl)	Germany	153.8	7.8	33
5	Home Depot	United States	151.2	9.8	3
6	The Kroger Co.	United States	140.0	3.5	1
7	JD.com	China	126.4	28.0	1
8	Walgreens Boots Alliance	United States	122.0	4.7	6
9	Aldi	Germany	120.9	4.8	19
10	Target	United States	104.6	8.5	1

Note: Carrefour (France) was excluded from the report at the company's request.
Source: Global Powers of Retailing 2023, Deloitte Report, https://www.deloitte.com/global/en/Industries/consumer/analysis/global-powers-of-retailing.html, accessed August 15, 2023.

In search of new opportunities, retailers have diversified not only across geographical market boundaries but also across product boundaries. First, most leading retailers have developed their own private-label product lines while simultaneously the products of leading national and international manufacturers. Second, retailers have increasingly adopted the discount format. As a result, more consumers are getting used to their streamlined, no-frills retail format. Third, retailers have also increasingly embraced the e-commerce format.[34]

Take a look at the world's largest discount store chain, Walmart of the United States. Walmart is now the largest company in the United States and the world's largest retailer, with annual retail revenues of about $573 billion in 2021. Walmart currently operates approximately 10 500 stores and clubs under 48 banners in 24 countries and e-commerce websites, and employs 1.6 million associates in the United States and 0.6 million associates outside the United States.[35] Walmart is Procter & Gamble's single-largest customer, buying as much as the household product giant sells to Japan. Walmart is extremely successful in the North American region but is not the largest global retailer, whereas 22 percent of its sales are generated outside its home market; the same figure for French retailer Carrefour is 50 percent.[36] Walmart's success is due to low tariffs in the USMCA zone, cheap labor and low-cost logistics, with savings passed on to consumers.

Despite its aggressive foreign expansion, Walmart experienced continued difficulties in markets such as Argentina, Brazil and Puerto Rico; and it pulled out of Germany, South Korea and Japan altogether. For example, in Brazil, Walmart's performance was lackluster, primarily due to its unwillingness to adapt to local market conditions; it eventually decided to withdraw from the Brazilian market by selling its Brazilian operations to private equity firm Advent International in 2018.[37] Similarly, Walmart sought to enter the challenging Japanese retail market in mid-2002 by acquiring Seiyu, Japan's fourth-largest supermarket group, paving the way for a low-cost strategy in Japan. However, Walmart's emphasis on

[34] Katrijn Gielens and Marnik G. Dekimpe, "Global Trends in Grocery Retailing," in Masaaki Kotabe and Kristiaan Helsen (eds.), *The SAGE Handbook of International Marketing* (London: SAGE Publications, 2009), pp. 413–28.
[35] Compiled from corporate.walmart.com, 2021.
[36] Compiled from corporate.walmart.com and carrefour.com, 2021.
[37] "Walmart brand to be dropped from supermarkets in Brazil," *Reuters*, www.reuters.com, August 12, 2019.

"Everyday Low Price" – the strategy that has worked for it in the United States – did not sit well with Japan's quality-conscious consumers, who associated "Everyday Low Price" with poor quality, or *"yasu-karou, waru-karou"* – "you get what you pay for." Take organic produce sold at Seiyu under Walmart's management as an example. The produce was advertised as low-priced "organic," indicating wholesomeness, but it had small marks and lacked uniformity in size and shape. As Japanese consumers tend to be less tolerant even of minor blemishes, they refused to buy the produce at Seiyu.[38] Consequently, Walmart suffered continued declining sales in Japan and was eventually forced to pull out of the market in 2020.[39]

Retailing involves very locally entrenched activities, including stocking an assortment of products that local consumers prefer; catering to local shopping patterns (e.g., shopping frequency, time of shopping and traffic jams) and seasonal promotions; and meeting local competition on a daily basis. International retailers that are willing to adapt their strategy to local ways of doing things while taking advantage of their managerial and IT capabilities seem to be more successful than those that try to "export" their ways of doing things to foreign countries. In general, European retailers tend to be more willing than U.S. or Japanese retailers to customize their marketing and procurement strategies to various local market peculiarities.[40]

For example, Carrefour approaches foreign markets differently. Having operated in the Chinese market since 1995 and developed a good understanding of Chinese consumers, the French retailer understands that Chinese consumers are eager to learn about Western products and has incorporated numerous signs that provide detailed product information in its supermarkets in China. For example, in the bakery department, Carrefour provides detailed explanations of the different flours used and their associated benefits. To promote French wine to consumers,

---

[38]   Hatakeyama Noboru, "Highly Demanding Japanese Consumers," *Japan Spotlight Bimonthly* 23, September/October 2004, 2–5; "Walmart to Make Seiyu A Group Company," NikkeiNet Interactive, www.nni.nikkei.co.jp, November 2, 2005.

[39]   "Walmart to Sell Majority Stake in Japan's Seiyu," *Supermarket News*, supermarketnews.com, November 16, 2020.

[40]   Brenda Sternquist, *International Retailing*, 2nd ed. (New York: Fairchild Publications, 2007).

Carrefour engaged a French wine specialist to provide advice and offer wine tastings to passing shoppers. The company became a clear market leader in Shanghai and other primary and secondary cities. At the end of 2017, Carrefour had 370 stores in China. In 2017, Carrefour opened its 20th hypermarket in Beijing, which is its largest store in Asia. There has been a major change in the food preferences of Chinese consumers. The new Carrefour store is designed to attract increasingly affluent Chinese consumers who are more quality conscious and prefer foreign-made quality products to domestic products. Located adjacent to Swedish home-furnishing retailer Ikea, the two-story Carrefour hypermarket – spanning approximately 11 534 square meters (m^2) (about 2.2 times the size of an American football field) – focuses on imported foodstuffs: it carries over 40 000 products, of which more than 6000 are imported. At the same time, Carrefour has started expanding its e-commerce business and rolling out its Easy Carrefour convenience store to diversify into retail formats that have been growing rapidly in China.[41] Easy Carrefour stores are about 500 m^2 and look like a typical convenience store or a compact supermarket. Carrefour also opened a brand-new store format, Carrefour Le Marche, in Shanghai. This new concept is a smart store with a French touch focused on catering and fresh imported products. Many of the digital innovations are supported by Tencent, China's leading provider of internet-related services and products.[42]

E-commerce and retailing

As e-commerce competition heats up, traditional bricks-and-mortar retailers have also boosted their online presence to attract consumers' attention and enhance their sales opportunities. The online market is

---

[41]   "Carrefour Online Store + Carrefour Easy Store," *Retail News Asia*, www .retailnews.asia, March 9, 2019.
[42]   "Carrefour Sees China as Testing Ground for New Retail Methods," *Reuters*, www.reuters.com, June 4, 2018.

increasingly crowded, complex and fragmented. As a result, many traditional retailers are utilizing various online models, including:

- directly operating their online storefront as a virtual version of their bricks-and-mortar stores (often described as "bricks-and-clicks" stores);
- offering their online storefront to third-party sellers as a marketplace;
- incorporating third-party marketplaces into their own online storefront;
- using social media for viral promotion; and
- selling products to other e-commerce retailers on a wholesale or consignment basis.

As online sales accelerate, especially in developing countries, traditional retailers are increasingly recognizing e-commerce as a key element of their global expansion strategies.

As a result, the e-commerce portion of traditional retailers' business has also increased. While Amazon still dominates the e-commerce market, with global sales of $469 billion in 2021, Walmart generated $75 billion in e-commerce sales that same year and is catching up in e-commerce sales. Clearly, e-commerce is becoming an increasingly dominant form of retailing, whether retailers started out as traditional bricks-and-mortar retailers (e.g., Walmart) or e-commerce retailers (e.g., Amazon).[43] In 2020, when the COVID-19 pandemic struck, online retailers such as Amazon and JD.com experienced the strongest growth, with sales rising by around one-third in one year alone. Most of the top 25 traditional retailers with existing e-commerce capability also increased their online sales by at least 50 percent, with five U.S.-based retailers seeing their online sales more than double.[44]

E-commerce is not limited to developed countries. China is already the fastest-growing internet market in Asia. The internet community in China has increased rapidly, soaring from 22.5 million users in 2000 to 989 million users in July 2020 – far beyond the United States' 312 million

---

[43] "2018 Global Powers of Retailing," Deloitte Report, 2018; "Amazon's Product Sales Climb Nearly 20% in 2018, but Only 8% in Q4," *Digital Commerce 360*, www.digitalcommerce360.com, January 31, 2019; ecommercedb.com.

[44] "Global Powers of Retailing 2023," Deloitte Report, 2021.

for the same year.[45] As a result of the unfortunate outbreak of severe acute respiratory syndrome in China in 2003, the Chinese government began to take advantage of the internet to encourage business transactions without unnecessary human contact. This government effort further helped build the internet market in China.[46] In Brazil, the number of people using the internet grew rapidly from 14 million in 2002 to 160 million by March 2021, making it South America's most wired nation and accounting for about half of the region's internet users.[47] A similar increase in the number of e-commerce operators is expected as internet access continues to grow.

One recent interesting phenomenon in e-commerce is the third-party marketplace. Retailers with e-commerce operations started providing links on their websites so that third-party sellers could sell their products either directly or on consignment. For example, more than 50 percent of Amazon's global sales in 2018 were accounted for by third-party sellers.[48]

As retailing essentially involves local activities directed at consumers, retailers must deal with local differences in tastes and preferences, as well as local peculiarities. Therefore, global retailers must address these local differences by localizing their offers and operations. By hosting third-party retailers to sell their own merchandise, e-marketplaces complement global retailers' responsiveness to the local market. Some online retailers embraced e-marketplaces from their start – notably Alibaba, which was founded in China in 1999, and Rakuten, which was founded in Japan in 1997.

Their business model is primarily to sell the e-marketplace as a service to third-party sellers, which can sell their own merchandise for a fee. Amazon – which started out as an online seller of books and other merchandise in 1995 – had to invest heavily in inventory, warehousing and distribution, resulting in a huge fixed investment. As a result, it took

---

[45]   Internet World Stats, www.internetworldstats.com.
[46]   "China Has World's 2nd Largest Number of Netizens," *XINHUA*, January 16, 2003; "China takes Steps to Ensure SARS Does Not Hinder Construction Plans," *XINHUA*, May 23, 2003.
[47]   Internet World Stats.
[48]   "Amazon's Product Sales Climb Nearly 20% in 2018, but Only 8% in Q4," *Digital Commerce 360*, www.digitalcommerce360.com, January 31, 2019.

many years to build a huge customer base before it became profitable.[49] On the other hand, Alibaba, Taobao and Tmall from China and Rakuten from Japan had limited fixed investment of their own, as they offered links on their web portals and third-party retailers selling on their websites had to shoulder the physical costs of inventory, warehousing, and distribution. These online marketplace companies were able to become profitable within a few years of founding. Two key features define an online marketplace:

• There are many sellers and buyers trading through the same website; and
• Buyers can purchase products without leaving the site (see Table 6.3 for a list of the top 10 online marketplace companies in the world).

As explained earlier in this chapter, despite the rapid increase in internet users and e-commerce participants around the world, the need for local or regional distribution of products remains as important today as it was before the internet revolution.

On-time retail information management

It may be tempting to cut down on stock in inventory in order to achieve cost savings. The chief reason for holding stock is to smooth out bumps in the supply chain. However, one of the biggest sources of inefficiency in logistics occurs exactly because distribution channel members do so independently of each other. This is known as the "bullwhip effect," so-called after how the amplitude of a whiplash increases down the length of the whip when it is cracked. Procter & Gamble discovered this effect more than a decade ago. The company noticed an odd thing about shipments of Pampers, its well-known brand of disposable diapers. Although the number of babies and the demand for diapers remained relatively stable, orders for Pampers fluctuated dramatically. This was because information about consumer demand can become increasingly distorted as it moves along the supply chain. For instance, when a retailer sees a slight increase in demand for diapers, it orders more from a wholesaler. The wholesaler then boosts its own sales forecast, causing the manufacturer to scale up production. But when the increase in demand turns out to

---

[49] "Amazon: Nearly 20 Years in Business and It Still Doesn't Make Money, But Investors Don't Seem to Care," *International Business Times*, www.ibtimes .com, February 13, 2014.

Table 6.3   The world's top 10 online marketplace companies

Rank	Company	Region/country	2021 visits/month (million)
1	Amazon	Global	5,200
2	eBay	Global	1,700
3	Mercado Libre	Latin America	683
4	Rakuten	Japan	576
5	AliExpress	Global	534
6	Shopee	Southeast Asia	458
7	Walmart.com	USA	410
8	Etsy	Global	392
9	Taobao	China	329
10	Pinduoduo	China	242

Source: "The World's Top Online Marketplaces 2021," *Webretailer*, https://www.webretailer.com/marketplaces-worldwide/online-marketplaces/.

be short-lived, the distribution channel is left with too much stock and orders are cut back.[50]

Computer systems can now tell a retailer instantly what it is selling in hundreds of stores across the world, how much money it is making on each sale and, increasingly, who its customers are. This has had two consequences, as discussed below.

Reduced inventory

First, a well-managed retailer need no longer keep large amounts of inventory – the stock burden has been passed upstream to the manufacturer. In addition, the retailer has a lower chance of running out of items. For a company such as Walmart, with more than 60 000 suppliers in the United States alone, keeping everyone informed is critical. The company does this through its Retail Link system, which suppliers can tap into over a secure internet connection. They can check stock levels and sales down

---

[50]   "Shining examples," *The Economist*, June 17, 2006, Special Section, pp. 4–6.

to the level of individual stores. Walmart may have a brutal reputation for driving down costs, but its investment in information systems has played a large part in building one of the world's most efficient supply chains, capable of handling more than $482 billion in annual sales. Another good example is 7-Eleven in Japan. The moment a 7-Eleven customer in Japan buys a soft drink or a can of beer, the information goes directly to the bottler or the brewery and is immediately input into the production schedule and the delivery schedule, specifying the hour at which the new supply must be delivered and to which of 7-Eleven's 20 700 stores in Japan. In effect, therefore, 7-Eleven controls the product mix, the manufacturing schedule and the delivery schedule of major suppliers such as Coca-Cola and Kirin Breweries. British retailer Sainsbury's supply chain is geared to provide inputs on demand from stores with a scheduled truck service to more than 1400 stores. The stores' ordering cycle is also set to match the loading and arrival of the trucks, which run almost according to a bus timetable.

Further attempts to reduce inventory can also be made jointly by retail chains for their mutual benefit. For example, in February 2000, Carrefour – joining the rush into the business-to-business e-commerce arena – announced a joint venture to build an online purchasing site through which retailers buy about $80 billion in combined purchases. The venture, called the WorldWide Retail Exchange, has created the industry's largest supply exchange on the internet. It is an e-business solution and service provider for the global retail industry. Suppliers can monitor retailers' sales, reduce inventory levels to a minimum and better plan the manufacturing of products on a hosted platform. The venture makes money by charging fees to suppliers and retailers that use the exchange and is set up as a separate entity with its own management, employees and financing.[51]

Market information at the retail level

Second, the retailer has real-time knowledge of what items are selling and how fast. This knowledge can be used to extract better terms from manufacturers. This trend in the transfer of power to the retailer in developed countries has coincided with the lowering of trade barriers around the world and the emergence of free-market economies in Asia and Latin America. As a result, retailers such as Walmart, Costco and Amazon in

---

[51]   "Worldwide Retail Exchange," *Crunchbase,* www.crunchbase.com.

the United States, Britain's Mark & Spencer and Sainsbury's, Mark in the Netherlands, Sweden's IKEA, France's Carrefour and Japan's 7-Eleven, Uniqlo and Muji are being transformed into global businesses.

A firm can use strong logistics capabilities as an offensive weapon to help gain competitive advantage in the marketplace by improving customer service and consumer choice, and by lowering the cost of global sourcing and finished goods distribution. These capabilities become increasingly important as the level of global integration increases and as competitors move to supplement low-cost manufacturing strategies in distant markets with effective logistics management strategies. This point is well illustrated by Ito-Yokado's takeover in 1991 of the Southland Corporation, which introduced 7-Eleven's convenience store concept to the United States and subsequently around the world. Seven & I (formerly Ito-Yokado) of Japan licensed the 7-Eleven store concept from Southland in the 1970s and invented just-in-time inventory management and revolutionized its physical distribution system in Japan. The key to Ito-Yokado's success with 7-Eleven Japan was the use of its inventory and physical distribution management systems to achieve lower on-hand inventory, faster inventory turnover and, most importantly, accurate information on customer buying habits. 7-Eleven Japan[52] now implements its just-in-time physical distribution system in 7-Eleven stores across the United States.[53]

Thus, distribution is increasingly becoming concentrated; manufacturing, by contrast, is splintering. Forty years ago, the Big Three automakers shared the U.S. auto market. Today, the market is split among fifteen car makers: Detroit's Big Three, five German companies, five Japanese companies and two Korean companies. Forty years ago, 85 percent of all retail car sales occurred in single-site dealerships; even three-dealership chains were uncommon. Today, a fairly small number of large-chain dealers account for 40 percent of car retail sales. In the United States, car buying is also moving online fast.[54]

---

[52]   The company is officially known as Seven-Eleven Japan owned by 7&i Holdings, while its stores are known as 7-Eleven stores.
[53]   Masaaki Kotabe, "The Return of 7-Eleven … from Japan: The Vanguard Program," *Columbia Journal of World Business,* 30, Winter 1995: 70–81.
[54]   "Online Car Sales Could Soon Be on Fast Track," *Automotive News,* www.autonews.com, February 6, 2017.

Given the increased bargaining power of distributors, monitoring their performance has become an important management issue for many multinationals. Although IT has improved immensely, monitoring channel members' performance remains a humanistic process. In general, companies that are less experienced in international operations tend to invest more resources in monitoring channel members' activities.[55] As they gain in experience, they increasingly build trusted relationships with channel members and depend more on formal performance-based control.[56]

Retailing differences across the world

The density of retail and wholesale establishments in different countries varies greatly. As a general rule, industrialized countries tend to have a lower distribution outlet density than emerging markets. Part of the reason for this difference stems from the need in emerging markets to purchase in very small lots and more frequently because of low income and the lack of facilities in homes to store and preserve purchased items. At the same time, the advanced facilities available in the developed world allow a much higher square footage of retail space per resident, due to the large size of retail outlets.

Japan's retail industry has a number of features that distinguish it from retailing in Western countries. They include a history of tight regulation – albeit that deregulation is increasing; less use of cars for shopping; and the importance of department stores in the lives of most people. For more than 40 years until recently, the Large-Scale Retail Store Law[57] in Japan helped to protect and maintain small retail stores (12 retail stores per 1000 residents in Japan, versus six retail stores per 1000 residents in the United States in 1994) and, partly in consequence, a multilayered distribution system. Consequently, Japan has experienced relatively limited prolif-

---

[55]   Esra F. Gencturk and Preet S. Aulakh, "The Use of Process and Output Controls in Foreign Markets," *Journal of International Business Studies,* 26, Fourth Quarter 1995: 755–86.

[56]   Preet S. Aulakh, Masaaki Kotabe and Arvind Sahay, "Trust and Performance in Cross Border Marketing Partnerships: A Behavioral Approach," *Journal of International Business Studies,* 27, Special Issue 1996: 1005–32.

[57]   Jack G. Kaikati, "The Large-Scale Retail Store Law: One of the Thorny Issues in the Kodak-Fuji Case," The American Marketing Association and the Japan Marketing Association Conference on the Japanese Distribution Strategy, November 22–24, 1998.

eration of megastores and large-scale shopping centers. Since Japan's urban areas are crowded, roads are congested and parking is expensive or nonexistent, many people use public transport to shop. Consequently, shopping usually takes place within a small radius of the home or work-place; and products, especially food, are generally bought in small quantities. Shopping, therefore, is more frequent. This trend is heightened by the requirements for fresh ingredients in Japanese cooking. Retail stores that not only stay open 24 hours a day throughout the week but also practice just-in-time delivery of fresh perishable foods, such as 7-Eleven and Lawson, are extremely popular in Japan. Even McDonald's recently introduced a motorcycle McDelivery service. Discount stores have also gained in popularity among recession-weary and newly price-conscious Japanese consumers. Similarly, department stores are a vital part of everyday Japanese life. The variety of goods and services offered by the average department store ranges well beyond that in most retail outlets abroad. Large department stores stock everything from fresh food and prepared dishes to discount and boutique clothing, and household and garden goods. Many have children's playgrounds and pet centers, some with displays resembling a miniature zoo. Museum-level art and craft exhibitions often are housed on upper floors, with both family and exqui-site restaurants usually on the top floor. This is a very different – and often difficult – market for foreign retailers to enter. See Global Viewpoint 6.1 for information on international retailers entering the Japanese market.

Global viewpoint 6.1: Foreign retailers and direct marketers enter Japan en masse

In Japan, up until the early 1990s, the Large-Scale Retail Store Law gave small retailers and wholesalers disproportionate influence over the Japanese market by requiring firms seeking to open a large store to submit their business plan to the local business regulation council, the local chamber of commerce (comprised the small retailers and whole-salers that would be affected) and the Ministry of Economy, Trade, and Industry (METI). The process generally took between one year and 18 months and was seen by foreign retailers as an almost insurmountable barrier to entry.

Under pressure from the U.S. government, the Large-Scale Retail Store

Law was relaxed in 1992 and 1994. Under the amendments, the task of examining applications for new stores was transferred from the local business regulation council to the Large-Scale Retail Store Council, a government advisory board under METI. Consequently, the maximum time required for various applications and approvals is now set at 12 months. These two revisions to the Large-Scale Retail Store Law have contributed to an increase in the number of applications requesting approval to establish a large retail store. According to the Japan Council of Shopping Centers, shopping centers have opened at a rate of more than 100 per year since 1992.

Toys "R" Us exploited this opportunity and ultimately succeeded in cracking the Japanese market. In 1996, it boasted a total of 37 stores in Japan. Following the success of Toys "R" Us, other foreign-based retailers have made forays into the Japanese market. Nearly a dozen other foreign retailers have opened their stores in Japan in the last two decades. Foreign firms face more difficulties when opening a general merchandise store than one for a niche product because the large Japanese general merchandise stores, such as Aeon and Ito-Yokado, are well entrenched and dominate the market. Despite the challenges, Walmart (United States) – which fully acquired Japan's struggling Seiyu – Carrefour (France) and Metro (Germany) all entered the Japanese market. However, their success was short-lived: Carrefour's early departure from the Japanese market was followed by Walmart's decision to pull out in 2020 and Metro's decision to withdraw in 2021. These developments highlight the difficulty of establishing foreign retail businesses in Japan. Specialty retailers of outdoor goods and clothes, including U.S.-based L.L. Bean and Eddie Bauer, have also poured into the Japanese market in the last 30 years. But while L.L Bean has carved a foothold in Japan, Eddie Bauer ended up closing all of its stores in Japan in 2021.

L.L. Bean and Eddie Bauer both teamed up with well-known Japanese companies. L.L. Bean Japan is a Japanese franchise, 70 percent of which is owned by Japan's largest retailing group, Seibu, and 30 percent by Panasonic. Eddie Bauer Japan was a joint venture between Otto-Sumitomo, a Sumitomo Group mail-order retailer, and Eddie Bauer USA. In general, establishing a joint venture or a franchise gives new market entrants a quicker start, although they risk losing control of operations in Japan. Future would-be entrants should bear in mind that Japan is not an easy place to do business, because regulations are extensive and stringent, and land and labor costs are extremely high.

On the other hand, direct marketing – another form of retailing – has blossomed into a $20-billion industry despite Japan's ongoing recession. Ten percent of this market belongs to foreign companies such as Lands' End, an outdoor clothing maker, and Intimate Brands, which distributes Victoria's Secret catalogs. "For those companies and individuals who say that Japan is a closed market, I really can't think of an example of an easier market entry than catalog sales," says Cynthia Miyashita, president of mail-order consultant Hemisphere Marketing Inc. in Japan. In high-context cultures like Japan, less direct, low-key approaches in which a mood or image is conveyed in an attempt to build a relationship with the audience are considered more appropriate ways to approach prospective customers than in low-context cultures such as the United States. Amway has also retained the leading position it has enjoyed in Japan for years. Amway not only focuses on direct selling activities but has also developed a physical presence in the market. This development of a physical environment in which consumers can experience products illustrates an important new trend in retailing: "customer experience" has become a buzzword as retailers seek to highlight points of difference from internet sales, which lack direct consumer access to products.

Foreign mail-order companies can sidestep Japan's notoriously complex regulations, multilevel distribution networks and even import duties. Here are a few cases in point:

- Japan's post offices are not equipped to impose taxes on the hundreds of thousands of mail-order goods that pass through the postal system, making direct marketing products virtually duty free. Local competitors that import products in bulk must pay duties, forcing up their prices.
- Many products, such as vitamins and cosmetics, are subject to strict testing regulations in Japan, but these rules do not apply if the products are sold through mail order for personal consumption. That gives mail-order customers in Japan access to a wide array of products that would otherwise be unavailable.
- Mail costs in the United States are so low that it is more economical to send a package from New York to Tokyo than from Tokyo to Osaka, which reduces overhead costs for direct-mail products.

- Although Japanese companies are not allowed to mail goods from foreign post offices for sale at home, foreign companies face no such restrictions.

Source: Joji Sakurai, "Firms Challenge Image of Japan's Closed Markets," *Marketing News*, July 20, 1998, p. 2; Jack G. Kaikati, "The Large-Scale Retail Store Law: One of the Thorny Issues in the Kodak-Fuji Case," in Michael R. Czinkota and Masaaki Kotabe (eds.), *Japanese Distribution Strategy* (London: Business Press, 2000), pp. 154-63; "Attitudes toward Direct Marketing and Its Regulation: A Comparison of the United States and Japan," *Journal of Public Policy & Marketing,* 19, Fall 2000: 228-37; "With Boots Firmly Planted in Japan, L.L. Bean Kicks Up Growth," *Portland Press Herald*, www.pressherald.com, November 19, 2018; "Walmart to Sell Majority Stake in Japan's Seiyu," *Supermarket News*, supermarketnews.com, November 16, 2020; "Eddie Bauer to Close All Stores in Japan," *Japan Times*, japantimes. co.jp, October 19, 2021.

Rules governing shopping hours, such as Sunday shopping, vary quite significantly around the world. In Germany, for example, opening hours have long been restricted through the *Ladenschlussgesetz* – a federal law regulating retail store hours which was first enacted in 1956 and most recently amended in 2003. The 2003 revision declared that stores must close on Sundays and public holidays. Stores were allowed to open from 6 a.m. until 8 p.m. on weekdays (Mondays to Fridays) and until 4 p.m. on Saturdays, with special rules applicable to Christmas Eve (December 24). However, in 2006, the federal government allowed states to pass their own laws to regulate store hours. Nevertheless, Sunday shopping is still mostly forbidden in Germany, although there are some exceptions such as at gas stations, airports, train stations and so forth. This situation is quite different from that in the United States, where retail stores can open seven days a week, 24 hours a day.[58] Keeping stores open in this manner requires very strong logistics management on the part of both retailers and the manufacturing firms that supply them. The sending organization, the receiving organization and the logistics provider (if applicable) must work very closely together.

In China, basket shopping is still considered the norm for most consumers. Retailers adjust their store layouts to cope with a large number of basket shoppers. Walmart, for instance, has set up basket-only checkouts in its supercenters to enable faster checkout. Because low prices afford the greatest competitive advantage, retailers disseminate strong price mes-

---

[58]   "Shopping Hours in Germany," *The German Way*, www.german-way.com.

sages throughout most of their stores in Chinese and English, highlighting both everyday low prices and promotions in both food and nonfood departments. As a result, high volumes of goods are heavily merchandised through major promotions in bins and in bulk floor stacks. In general, a store flyer is a key marketing tool, designed to drive foot traffic by presenting discounts for household commodities. Recent research revealed the following key differences between hypermarkets in China and those in the West:

The majority of hypermarkets in China are located on two floors, with nonfood items located on the upper floor and food on the lower floor.

- Many hypermarkets in China are located inside shopping centers in the heart of the city.
- Chinese hypermarkets have high staffing levels due to the presence of suppliers' staff working as in-store "merchandisers."
- Chinese retailers provide courtesy buses to bring customers from residential areas into the city center because China has low car ownership.[59]

Summary

Logistics or supply chain management traditionally involved a series of local measures aimed at getting goods to the end customer in a local market. However, while the aim of serving the customer remains, retailers have been transformed into global organizations that buy and sell products from and to many parts of the world. At the same time, with the increased globalization of manufacturing, many firms are optimizing their worldwide production by sourcing components and raw materials from around the world. Both of these trends have increased the importance of global logistics management for firms.

Logistics management is closely linked to manufacturing activities and is increasingly being outsourced to 3PL specialists. Many companies – particularly in the EU – are trying to develop consolidated production locations so that they can reduce the number of distribution centers and

---

[59]   "Retailing in China," *Retail Analysis*, iReports, www.igd.com/analysis.

market their products from a small number of locations throughout Europe. Firms such as Federal Express, DHL and TNT have evolved from document shippers to providers of complete logistics functions; indeed, all of these firms now have a business logistics division whose function is to handle the outsourced logistics functions of corporate clients.

Many governments have developed FTZs, export processing zones and other special economic zones designed chiefly to increase domestic employment and exports from the zones. Various tax and other cost benefits available in FTZs entice both domestic and foreign firms to set up warehousing and manufacturing operations there.

When it comes to international distribution, managers need to make careful decisions on how to configure their distribution channel. Issues such as cost, coverage and control determine how many intermediaries there should be and where. Ongoing management of the distribution channel can be a challenge, with channel conflict an ever-present issue for many international marketing managers.

Retail has long been considered a fairly localized activity subject to different customer needs and different national laws regulating domestic commerce. Nevertheless, significant changes are taking place in the retail sector. IT makes it increasingly easy for large retailers to know what they are selling in hundreds of stores around the world. Given this intimate knowledge of customers globally, retailers have begun to assume the channel leadership role from manufacturers.

Finally, e-commerce is increasingly dispensing with the need for physical stores. However, local adaptation of product offerings and the establishment of local distribution centers remain as important today as they were before the internet revolution. Furthermore, complex international shipping requirements and exchange rate fluctuations can hinder the smooth distribution of products around the world.

7 Global supply chain management for sustainability[1]

Introduction

Global supply chains have played a critical role in the growth and development of world trade and the integration of business operations on a worldwide scale. As stated previously, one of the primary objectives of global supply chain management is to develop a cost-efficient delivery mechanism.

In recent decades, however, two prominent issues facing global supply chain management have motivated many scholars and practitioners to rethink its role in our ever-changing world. First, the development of world trade over the years has also made us aware of the degradation of the environment on a global scale through increased marine pollution from discarded plastics and climate change due to the increased use of fossil fuels, among other things. The sustainability of our lifestyle as we know it is increasingly being questioned, giving rise to corporate sustainability issues resulting from concerns over the negative impact of industrial activities on the natural environment and society in general. The threats to the wellbeing of our current generation, and the prospects of leaving a grim legacy for future ones, have led many to demand greater accountability from firms whose actions cause detriment to society and the environment.[2]

---

[1]   This chapter is based on a position paper on sustainable supply chain management requested from the editor of the *Journal of Sustainable Marketing* and builds on Masaaki Kotabe, "Thoughts on Sustainable Business, Circular Economy, and Circular Supply Chain Management," *Journal of Sustainable Marketing*, 4(1), April 24, 2023: 1–8.
[2]   Martin Wolf, *The Crisis of Democratic Capitalism* (New York: Penguin Random House, 2023).

Second, the upsurge in global supply networks in recent decades, resulting from the widespread adoption of global outsourcing practices by firms seeking to reduce costs in a more competitive and globalized business environment, has shifted stakeholder focus from the individual firm to its supply network. The argument is that in a context where global supply networks have become ubiquitous, corporate sustainability cannot be constrained to the corporate boundaries of an individual firm but must encompass the entire value chain of its products.[3] This shift in stakeholder focus has increased the prominence and relevance of sustainable supply chain management among practitioners, academics and the media.[4]

The need for a shift to a circular economy for sustainability

At the fundamental level, supply chain management as we know it today is based on a "linear economy" paradigm (i.e., make, use and dispose), in which the primary role of firms is to develop, manufacture and distribute products downstream to final consumers at a minimum total cost. The disposal of those products after their service life is not woven into supply chain management thought. Historically, this issue was critically addressed in classic works such as Thornstein Veblen's *The Theory of the Leisure Class* (1899) and the Club of Rome's *The Limits to Growth* (1972). While these raised the issue of sustainability, they never came close to providing potential solutions. However, in 1977, Walter Stahel and Geneviève Ready-Mulvey advocated the idea of a "circular economy" paradigm (i.e., make, reuse, remake and recycle) in a report to the European Commission, which was later expanded and published as a book, *Jobs for Tomorrow* (1981). A circular economy turns products that are at the

---

[3]   Daniel R. Krause, Stephan Vachon and Robert D. Klassen, "Special Topic Forum on Sustainable Supply Chain Management: Introduction and Reflections on the Role of Purchasing Management," *Journal of Supply Chain Management*, 45(4), 2009: 18–25.

[4]   Bruno Barreto de Góes, Masaaki Kotabe and José Mauricio Galli Geleilate, "The Diffusion of Corporate Sustainability in Global Supply Networks: An Empirical Examination of the Global Automotive Industry," in Alain Verbeke, Rob Van Tulder, Elizabeth L. Rose and Yingqi Wei (eds.), *The Multiple Dimensions of Institutional Complexity in International Business Research*, Vol. 15 (Bingley: Emerald Publishing Limited, 2021), 435–58.

end of their service life into resources for others by creating a closed-loop industrial system to minimize resource inputs and reduce waste, pollution and carbon emissions.[5] Circular systems employ reuse, sharing, repair, refurbishing, remanufacturing and recycling to improve resource sustainability in industrialized economies. This is a powerful proposition.

To ensure that the circular economy paradigm is viable, however, stakeholders in the globally dispersed supply chain must collectively manage resources (i.e., materials, components and finished products) by reusing, refilling, reprogramming, repairing, remanufacturing and upgrading for improved efficiency. Let us call this effort "circular supply chain management."

For the purposes of this chapter, corporate sustainability in circular supply chain management is addressed in terms which correspond to the concept of the triple bottom line, as conceived of by John Elkington in 1998,[6] and which were subsequently expanded into the 17 Sustainable Development Goals (SDGs) of the United Nations (UN).[7] This concept moves away from a purely economic view of a firm's purpose toward a perspective that takes into consideration the firm's environmental and social impacts, and consequently its duties in relation to those additional dimensions. Hence, "corporate sustainability" is defined by firms' collective actions, behaviors and initiatives that consider economic, social and environmental performance as inextricably connected.[8] However, the emergence of pervasive global supply networks and the disaggregation of value chains also imply that the establishment of seamless circular supply chains is no longer the result of individual stakeholders, but rather of networks of organizations that span national boundaries, with each responsible for a share of that collective goal.

---

5   Walter R. Stahel, "The Circular Economy," *Nature*, www.nature.com, 531, 2016: 435–38.

6   John Elkington, *Cannibals with Forks: The Triple Bottom Line of the 21st Century* (Stoney Creek, CT: New Society, 1998).

7   Ben Purvis, Mao Yong and Robinson Darren, "Three Pillars of Sustainability: In Search of Conceptual Origins," *Sustainability Science*, 14, 2019: 681–95.

8   Craig R. Carter and Dale S. Rogers, "A Framework of Sustainable Supply Chain Management: Moving Toward New Theory," *International Journal of Physical Distribution and Logistics Management*, 38(5), 2008: 360–87.

The proponents of sustainable marketing also stress such resource management must be market-driving, not just market-driven. Therefore, sustainability issues should be driven not only by the needs and wants of environmentally mindful consumers, but also by stakeholder firms in conjunction with active government participation at the local, national and international levels through setting goals, policies, laws and regulations to effect behavioral change and shape economic activities that affect the environment and society.[9]

Circular supply chain management: still a distant dream

A circular economy could be achieved if a functioning circular supply chain were made possible through the collective actions of stakeholders creating a closed-loop industrial system with appropriate oversight and regulation by government agencies. However, that seems much easier said than done.

Take the case of long-running simple recycling programs for aluminum cans, glass and polyethylene terephthalate (PET) bottles and plastic waste around the world. Beverage cans are the global leader in recycling efforts. For example, aluminum can recycling rates are generally high in many countries, as the recycling statistics for 2020–22 bear out (Japan 97 percent; Germany 99 percent; Finland 98 percent; United Kingdom 82 percent; Italy 67 percent; Spain 56 percent; France 45 percent; United States 45 percent).[10] By contrast, the glass bottle recycling rate for the

---

[9]   Jagdish N. Sheth and Atul Parvatiyar (2021), "Sustainable Marketing: Market-Driving, Not Market-Driven," *Journal of Macromarketing*, 41(1), 150–65, https://doi.org/10.1177/0276146720961836.

[10] "Recycling Rate of Aluminum Cans in Europe in 2020, by country," *Statista*, www.statista.com, 2023; "Can to Can Recycling Rate of Aluminum Cans Japan FY 2012-2021," *Statista*, www.statista.com, 2023; "New Analysis Shows Significant Economic and Environmental Benefits of Boosting Aluminum Can Recycling Rate in U.S.," *PR Newswire*, March 30, 2022, www.prnewswire.com/news-releases/new-analysis-shows-significant-economic-and-environmental-benefits-of-boosting-aluminum-can-recycling-rate-in-us-301513888.html#:~:text=Notably%2C%20while%20the%20Aluminum%20Association,occur%20during%20collection%20and%20sorting.

United States is just 33 percent, compared to 90 percent in Switzerland and Germany and 69 percent in Japan.[11] When it comes to PET bottles, Norway has the highest recycling rate, at 97 percent; this is followed by Japan at 85 percent, the EU at 58 percent, and the United States trailing behind at only 29 percent.[12] Although one single statistical source is not available, there are significant divergences in overall regular plastic waste recycling rates, which stand at 86 percent in Japan, 33 percent in the EU and a meager 5 percent in the United States.[13] Although direct comparisons should be made with caution, given some measurement differences among the three regions, these divergences in regular plastic waste recycling rates appear staggering. They are not necessarily the result of a lack of technical know-how, but rather due to a lack of functioning regulatory governance by national and local governments, as well as attitudes of firms and consumers toward recycling.

The overall recycling rates for the easiest-to-recycle products not only are far below 100 percent, but also vary significantly across countries and regions. In general, the Nordic countries, Germany and Japan have very high overall recycling rates, while the United States lags significantly behind. One might naturally expect that the more complex the products and components (e.g., computer motherboards), the more difficult it would be to refurbish, reuse and recycle them. However, an increasing number of companies are now outlining strategies aimed at embracing a circular economy. Decisions to reuse, refurbish, remanufacture or recycle go a long way toward improving sustainable supply chain operations and building a circular economy. However, the fact remains that for those items that cannot be salvaged in one way or another, close to 40

---

[11] "Picking up the Pieces of US Glass Recycling," *Chemical & Engineering News*, February 11, 2019, https://cen.acs.org/magazine/97/09706.html; "Recycling Rate of Glass Bottles in Japan from 2018 to 2020," *Statista*, 2003, www.statista.com.

[12] "PET Plastic Bottle Recycling Rates in Select Countries as of 2018," *Statista*, 2023, www.statista.com.

[13] "Recycling Rate of Plastic Waste in Japan from 2011 to 2020," *Statista*, 2022, www.statista.com; "Plastics and Circularity – Closing the Plastic Loop: Can New Technologies Accelerate Plastic Recycling in Europe?" *The Economist*, www.economist.com, December 20, 2021; "US is Recycling Just 5% of its Plastic Waste, Studies Show," *The Guardian*, www.theguardian.com, May 5, 2022.

percent are still discarded rather than recycled.[14] To build a truly circular supply chain, companies and suppliers must commit to reusing, refurbishing, remanufacturing and recycling.

For example, refurbishing parts gives components a new lease of life and restores them to their original factory condition, meaning their quality and lifespan should be identical to those of a brand-new part. Refurbished parts can contribute significantly to the circular economy, maintaining efficiency and shortening lead times. However, a 2017 GEODIS worldwide supply chain survey revealed that 62 percent of companies had limited visibility into their supply chains; and 15 percent had visibility into production only and thus experienced difficulties in sourcing and quality assuring refurbished components.[15]

However, one promising recent development in this regard is Toyota's RESCUE (REinforce Supply Chain Under Emergency) program, which aims to:

- make the procurement network "visible" from first to third suppliers all the way to tenth suppliers on a global basis;
- classify components between one and eight categories according to differences in supply disruption risk; and
- assess high-risk components together with suppliers for alternative procurement methods and a stable supply path.

Although RESCUE was developed to deal with global supply chain disruptions caused by natural calamities such as earthquakes and extreme weather events, the program is designed to make visible alternative quality-assured sources for disrupted supplies.[16]

Technical difficulties in the supply chain management side are an issue which can multiply in magnitude once different countries with different laws and regulations are taken into account. Add in consumers' varying levels of commitment to recycling and the achievement of a functioning

---

[14] "The Circular Supply Chain: A Push for Sustainability," *Forbes*, July 29, 2021, www.forbes.com.

[15] Sven Bretschneider, "Circular Supply Chain Can Ease Manufacturing Problems," *SupplyChain*, July 2, 2022, www.supplychaindigital.com.

[16] "How Toyota Kept Making Cars When the Chips Were Down," *Fortune*, August 1, 2021, www.fortune.com.

circular supply chain appears more like a distant dream than a reality, despite its societal appeal in addressing various environmental concerns regarding sustainability. According to two leading authorities on circular supply chain management, the primary reason for a lack of functioning examples is that successful circular supply chains tend to be quite localized and the products and services involved comprise a relatively limited number of simple components.[17] In reality, most manufactured products have the opposite properties, involving many specialized parts with complex alloys and highly dispersed supply chain operations across national boundaries in order to optimize a performance-cost tradeoff. Consequently, circular supply chains remain inherently difficult to achieve based on profit incentives alone. Although proponents of sustainable marketing may argue that consumers should be educated on the importance of circular supply chains for sustainability, one also wonders how willing consumers would be to compromise on performance and cost.

Where do we go from here?

One thing is clear: the invisible hand of the free market economy alone is not sufficient to achieve a circular economy. The interdependence of self-interested individual stakeholders in the free market economy cannot in itself incentivize suppliers and manufacturers, as well as consumers, to do what is socially necessary. The environment has long been taken for granted as a public good and individual stakeholders are not willing to pay an added price to protect it. Since it is a public good, government intervention is needed.

At a macro level, various governments, in conjunction with international institutions such as the UN, may need to develop global standards for component and product specifications in much the same way as patents are harmonized across different countries so as to align laws and procedures among intellectual property systems to ensure consistency and

---

[17]   Khaled Soufani and Christoph Loch, "Circular Supply Chains Are More Sustainable. Why Are They So Rare?" *Harvard Business Review*, June 15, 2021, https://hbr.org/2021/06/circular-supply-chains-are-more-sustainable-why-are-they-so-rare.

clarity of rights for the world's innovators. Technical harmonization introduced in 2020 in the automobile sector in the EU – known as the Whole Vehicle Type-Approval System (WVTA) – is a step in the right direction. Under the WVTA, an auto manufacturer can obtain certification for a vehicle type in one member state and market it throughout the EU without further tests. The European Commission is responsible for legislating on automobiles and setting rules on safety and environmental protection; it is also responsible for the approval and market surveillance of automobiles, systems, components and separate technical units.[18] However, while this regime may encourage auto manufacturers to improve the acceptability of components and other technical units across EU member states, it falls short of establishing rules on their convertibility or standardization. Such global standard-setting efforts could enable component suppliers and manufacturers to improve the interchangeability of materials and components and reduce unnecessary waste and redundancies in the supply chain.

Another standard-setting effort is the new carbon pricing framework developed and ratified by the EU. Through this framework, EU member states have collectively agreed to regulate industrial carbon emissions.[19] Firms operating in the EU must abide by the carbon pricing rules set forth by the EU authorities. One of the major reasons why Japan generally has much higher recycling rates for aluminum cans and glass and PET bottles as well as plastic waste than the United States is its overarching Container and Packaging Recycling Act (CPRA), which was enacted in 1995, came into force in 1997 and was further revised and updated in 2006; and which imposes specific recycling mandates on firms.[20] By contrast, the United

---

[18]   European Commission, "Technical Harmonisation," Internal Market, Industry, Entrepreneurship and SMEs, https://single-market-economy.ec .europa.eu/sectors/automotive-industry.

[19]   Richard J. Albert and Alwyn Hopkins, "The New EU Carbon Pricing Framework and Its Impact for Business," *Bloomberg Tax*, February 6, 2023, https://news.bloombergtax.com/daily-tax-report-international/the-new-eu -carbon-pricing-framework-and-its-impact-for-business.

[20]   The CPRA promotes recycling in cooperation with the government, municipalities, consumers and business enterprises, and proactively supports and coordinates partnerships between these parties. It applies to all medium- to large-scale business entities that manufacture, use, import or sell containers or wrapping. The law provides for a collaborative system according to the principle that all parties in society – including business entities (manufacturers and users), municipal governments and consumers – should collabo-

States has no federal regulations on recycling; instead, each state has its own separate regulations, with inconsistent levels of enforcement.

However, a question remains as to whether well-enforced government regulations would suffice in themselves to improve the rate of conformity by both firms and consumers. Some fundamental divergences in the level of conformity could well be due to cultural differences, which are well known to affect consumer behavior.[21] It would be interesting to see how consumers in different countries react to social issues such as recycling.

More research in the comparative public policy arena across different countries and regions is also needed. For example, one recent Japanese study on the effects of the CPRA revealed that, in addition to policies targeted at households, policies targeted at municipalities have played an important role in facilitating the recycling of post-consumer plastic waste.[22] The enforcement of national laws at the local level may be more effective than enforcement at the national level. If so, what policy implications could this have for the lackluster recycling results in the United

---

rate in realizing the rational and efficient recycling of waste containers and packaging. Actual oversight and implementation of recycling efforts are executed at each municipality government level by the Japan Containers and Packaging Recycling Association, a government-designated organization. The volume of recyclable materials handled by each business is estimated annually and the total cost of recycling those materials is projected by the municipal government in collaboration with businesses. If the total amount of recycling expenses that is actually required falls below the total amount of expenses initially projected for each business, specified business entities must pay a monetary amount equivalent to half of the difference in expenses as "payment for rational recycling" to the municipal government. For practical purposes, (half of) the unrealized recycling expenses are treated as a penalty allocated to specific businesses. Therefore, businesses are encouraged to comply with the recycling law by implementing various methods to collect recyclable materials from consumers. For more details, see Ministry of Economy, Trade and Industry, Japan, the Containers and Packaging Recycling Law, 2003.

[21] David A. Griffith, Salih Tamer Cavusgil and Shichun Xu, "Emerging Themes in International Business Research," *Journal of International Business Studies,* 39, 2008: 1220–35.

[22] Yuichi Ishimura, "The Effects of the Containers and Packaging Recycling Law on the Domestic Recycling of Plastic Waste: Evidence from Japan," *Ecological Economics,* 201, November 2022: https://doi.org/10.1016/j.ecolecon.2022.107535.

States, where recycling laws are enacted at the state level, without any uniform federal regulations?

In a similar vein, the macro role of international institutions such as the UN, the International Monetary Fund (IMF) and the World Bank should be considered. Clearly, the SDGs have a role to play in encouraging recycling and ultimately realizing the idea of circular supply chains. However, making concerted efforts to contribute to the SDGs is no easy task at the national level, particularly in many developing countries. For example, the IMF is known to have successfully allocated funds to direct developing countries' efforts to address certain structural weaknesses in their infrastructure for further economic development.[23] Therefore, the role that the IMF could play in improving recycling in developing countries should equally be explored. In a similar vein, the World Bank could offer seed financing to leading recycling firms in developed countries to transfer expertise to developing countries through foreign direct investment.

Finally, at a micro level, one of the major characteristics of today's supply chain is its dispersed nature. No stakeholder is singly in charge of establishing its supply chain; instead, today's supply chains comprise a multiplicity of stakeholders. It is uncertain whether functioning circular supply chains can be developed with so many diverse stakeholders involved, with different profit and other motives. Similarly, it is uncertain whether a lead firm is needed as a champion (or platform leader) of the cause, to manage the various interactions between stakeholders in a supply chain. If so, additional research will be needed on effective ways to identify and empower such platform leaders.[24]

Regardless of the levels of research implied above, technology – and particularly information technology – is changing fast. It will equally be

---

[23] Sam C. Okoroafo and Masaaki Kotabe, "The IMF's Structural Adjustment Program and Its Impact on Firm Performance: A Case of Foreign and Domestic Firms in Nigeria," *Management International Review*, 33(2), 1993: 139–56.

[24] Bruno Barreto de Góes, Masaaki Kotabe and José Mauricio Galli Geleilate, "The Diffusion of Corporate Sustainability in Global Supply Networks: An Empirical Examination of the Global Automotive Industry," in Alain Verbeke, Rob Van Tulder, Elizabeth L. Rose and Yingqi Wei (eds.), *The Multiple Dimensions of Institutional Complexity in International Business Research*, Vol. 15 (Bingley: Emerald Publishing Limited, 2021), pp. 435–58.

interesting to see how new advancements such as platform-as-a-service (PaaS) and mobility-as-a-service (MaaS) could facilitate the necessary changes and coordination among dispersed stakeholders at both the macro and micro levels. PaaS is a complete development and deployment environment in the cloud, with resources that make it possible for stakeholders to deliver everything from simple cloud-based apps to sophisticated, cloud-enabled enterprise applications. MaaS is a type of service that, through a joint digital channel, enables stakeholders to plan, book and pay for multiple types of supply chain services. The concept describes a shift away from individually owned modes of logistics toward mobility provided as a service. Such systems combine supply chain services from public and private logistics providers through a unified gateway that creates and manages the entire supply chain.[25]

The bottom line is that there is no returning to the old ways of doing things in the linear economy of the past. If we are serious about sustainability in the face of environmental degradation and climate change, governments, firms and consumers will all have to embrace a circular economy in which we collectively strive to reduce waste and reuse scarce resources for our common good.

Summary

This chapter illustrates the need for firms to address resource sustainability to combat the negative impacts of environmental degradation and climate change. It suggests that the industry should move from the linear economy to the circular economy, with recyclability built into all economic activities.

---

[25] Ursula Rauchecker, Matthias Meier, Ralf Muckenhirn, Arthur Yip, Ananda Jagadeesan and Jonathan Corney, "Cloud-Based Manufacturing-as-a-Service Environment for Customized Products," *eChallenges e-2011 Conference Proceedings*, IIMC International Information Management Corporation, 2011; Gongtao Zhang, Bart L. MacCarthy and Dmitry Ivanov, "The Cloud, Platforms, and Digital Twins – Enablers of the Digital Supply Chain," in Bart L. MacCarthy and Dmitry Ivanov (eds.), *The Digital Supply Chain* (Amsterdam: Elsevier, 2022), pp. 77–91.

However, this chapter also highlights how difficult it is to implement circular supply chain management in practice. Greater coordination among all participants in the supply chain is required. Furthermore, both international and domestic governing institutions will need to play a role in making the circular economy a reality. While we are moving in the right direction, more coordinated efforts are needed on a global basis.

Index